UNLEASHING FIREPOWER

MASTERS OF BUSINESS EXCELLENCE

COACH M J TOLAN

Before we get started, a few acknowledgements

Special Buckets of Thanks to:

Our Amazing Editor Dr. Randi D. Ward

Communications Coordinator Vilma Mantilla

To 'The Great 8,' The Tolan Brothers for their constant support,

To all of our Volunteers of our NGO Time 4 sharing over the years, special kudos to the Ranara and Manago families.

To Vivo, LX, and NG

All of my great mentors, many of whom co-wrote the book with me.

To Ben Gay III who wrote not only 'The Closers' but also the original book on success and humility, all my respect and appreciation.

Angelica Kristina Tolan for your invaluable and timely input!

To my LinkedIn Tribe of supporters, many of you who are now dear friends … L P H

and last but never the least, Our Lord God who gave me the strength and courage to send cancer back to the curb…. to all my great healthcare givers who tolerated me holding my laptop while writing this project in the hospital when they needed to give me an IV or check BP post-surgery.

"Never lose your sense of humor, if you do, someone else might find it and actually believe they are funny…" Dashi

To everyone who sent me prayers of support during my health journey, Thank you…

God is Great, Amen!

"They thought they had buried me, but never knew I was a seed."

CONTENTS

A Foreword by Ben Gay III

Author of The Closers 1, 2, & 3

Ben Gay III has been called a living legend in the sales world. After 50+ years in professional selling, he has been the #1 salesperson in every organization in which he has worked. At age 25 he was president of what was then the world's largest direct sales/network marketing company, having been personally trained by fellow sales legends J. Douglas Edwards, Dr. Napoleon Hill, Earl Nightingale, William Penn Patrick, Zig Ziglar and many other sales giants.

One of the most famous, popular, and powerful sales trainers in the world, Ben now writes/publishes/produces "The Closers" series of books/audios/videos/newsletters/podcasts/live seminars, a series that is considered to be "The Foundation of Professional Selling."

Ben was the founder and is the current Executive Director of The National Association of Professional Salespeople. Ben and his lovely wife Gigi live near Lake Tahoe in the little Northern California town of Placerville, California – where the California Gold Rush began!

"For any entrepreneur, the race to stay relevant amidst new trends and emerging methodologies can sometimes feel like a never-ending marathon.

Yet, as overwhelming as it can be, the flames of innovation and growth must always be stoked, lest they wane.

It's with this thought in mind that I am privileged to introduce you to "Unleashing Firepower, Masters of Business Excellence" by Coach MJ Tolan and a remarkable ensemble of co-authors.

To state it simply, this isn't just another business book; it's a manual, a guide, and perhaps most importantly, a testament to the human spirit's indomitable will to succeed.

As you delve into the pages of this work, each chapter unfolds like a mosaic, letting you gaze into the vast expertise and experience of the authors.

Their stories, lessons, and insights aren't just didactic; they're profoundly relatable. These co-authors bring their own flare, their unique vantage point, but if there's one golden thread that weaves them all together, it's undoubtedly the concept of 'Mind Set.'

Mindset isn't just a word; it's the foundational bedrock upon which all success is built.

Your perspective on challenges, be they grand or minuscule, shapes the trajectory of your endeavors.

And as I've always believed, the right attitude isn't just a catalyst for success in business but a compass for life itself.

In my fledgling years, seeking knowledge wasn't just a passion; it was a lifeline.

I was fortunate to cross paths with towering figures who had not only mastered their craft but were eager to impart their wisdom.

One such luminary was Dr. Napoleon Hill, the maestro behind the masterpiece, "Think and Grow Rich." The indelible mark he left on me is something I cherish every day. Dr. Hill taught me personally as my personal mentor that our potential isn't confined by our circumstances, but rather, it's boundless, limited only by the scope of our imagination and the tenacity of our belief.

"Unleashing Firepower, Masters of Business Excellence" stands as a beacon, nudging every entrepreneur, every dreamer, to look within and recognize the latent power they possess.

It prompts us to harness that potential, to embrace the ever-changing world of business with both arms and to mold it with our vision.

In conclusion, I implore every reader, whether a seasoned business magnate or a young budding entrepreneur, to approach this book not just as a source of knowledge, but as a mirror reflecting your own untapped potential. Let it be the spark that ignites your inner fire and propels you to realms of excellence hitherto unimagined.

Allow the Co-Authors, these 'Masters of Business Excellence' experts, to be your mentors and guides.

Who knows, they just might light a spark that could propel your journey onward into opportunities never imagined before.

Here's to putting their Firepower to work for you."

— Ben Gay III

Unleashing Firepower: Masters of Business Excellence

"In a world that spins faster with every tick of the clock, where the line between genius and madness is sometimes measured with the stroke of a pen, a solitary idea can ignite the engines of enterprise and awaken dormant giants."

Imagine for a moment—Steve Jobs in his garage, crafting the blueprint of Apple with the alchemy of foresight and audacity; Walt Disney with a pencil and a dream, turning doodles into realms of wonder that would captivate humanity.

These architects of extraordinary didn't merely play the game; they reinvented it, one audacious move at a time. You, the would-be pioneer, the corporate maverick, the startup visionary—you are not alone.

My name is Michael Tolan aka 'Coach M J. Tolan,' and I am delighted to introduce the 'Masters of Business Excellence' that you will meet in this book.

I have started several successful businesses on my own, divesting one that yielded over 100,000,00 Million USD in sales, which is mere peanuts to what I might have done by taking advice from any one of these Co-authors.

They are all extraordinary professionals who will guide you through their own wheelhouse in order to drop golden nuggets for you to take straight into the office or the boardroom.

Ahead of you lies a treasure trove of wisdom that draws its lineage from former military leaders, neuroscientists, corporate trainers and experts on Ai.

Here, the realms of logic and intuition dance in a ballet of influence and insight.

Welcome to 'Unleashing Firepower: Masters of Business Excellence.'

Prepare yourself for an odyssey that defies conventional wisdom, challenging boundaries between disciplines that seem worlds apart but are intrinsically tied to business excellence.

Each chapter ahead is a treasure map, refined through experience, polished by practice, and embedded into the crown of mastery to enable readers to formulate a winning strategy in business today.

Pay close attention to the insights shared by the Masters of Business Excellence, including a battle plan from a three-star General as he presents a masterful strategy, not just as a sequence of maneuvers in a war room but as a holistic concept that translates into the world of operational business.

Check out the findings from a top data analyst who demonstrates that numbers, like words, have stories to tell and prophecies to fulfill.

Dive into the mind sciences with a top C-level executive coach and neuroscientist, unraveling the intricate connections between performance and untapped potential.

Ever wondered how the grit, tenacity, and adaptability ingrained in a Navy SEAL could metamorphose into becoming an entrepreneur?

Prepare to be enlightened.

Witness a new breed of business leadership insights in its brightest and darkest shades. Learn why teams, the building blocks of any organization, often crumble like houses of cards. Learn how teams can instead become fortresses of ingenuity.

Understand the subtle yet commanding role of emotional intelligence in today's automated world and discover the magnetic force of talent—how to attract it, cultivate it, and maintain it.

Insights from our top consultants and speakers on the power of mastering Emotional Intelligence, which is proving to be one of the most sought-after qualities and skills in CEOs today, are shared.

Take a journey into a 'Masterclass on Leadership' curated by a retired Captain in the United States Navy and former presidential advisor.

Get a chance to level up your end game and become a sought-after 'thought leader' to get speaking gigs on stage by one of the world's top C-level branding coaches and award-winning motivational speakers.

You stand at the threshold of a grand hall of wisdom, your path lit by the legends who've not just walked but soared and revolutionized their traversed avenues.

This is not just a book; it is an arsenal of business ammunition.

An arsenal designed to arm you with the multidimensional skills, tactics, and perspectives you need to navigate the world of modern business.

So, are you ready to unleash the firepower necessary to ignite your business growth?

In the commotion of life's demands and the pursuit of success, there exists a well-kept secret sauce which is the essence of entrepreneurial leadership.

We are told that the entrepreneurial leader role is the pinnacle of hierarchy in the corporate world, the position of choice for CEOs and captains of industries. However, the reality of it is that the essence of true leadership transcends these boundaries, revealing itself as a guiding light of behaviors and practices in our daily lives.

Leadership development is not only in business but in every role we play in our lives, impacting and influencing the lives of others.

Unleashing Firepower is for the open-minded leaders who are receptive to the wisdom shared by individuals from all walks of life who have walked the walk.

Within these pages, you will find a collection of perspectives, resources, and timeless principles presented by a diverse array of voices.

These exceptional individuals, each offering their distinct insights, will guide you on a transformative journey towards becoming a better business leader not only in your professional endeavors but in the very core of your being.

As you set forth on this journey, you will confront not only the triumphs but also the trials, the adversities within leadership often overlooked. It is our hope that this book will not only equip you with the tools and tips to excel in your business goals but also serve as a compass to navigate the pitfalls.

So, whether you aspire to lead a Fortune 500 company, a startup, a family, or simply your own life's journey, remember that the wisdom contained here will help illuminate your path.

In the chapters that follow, you will discover the essence of business leadership – the bravery to lead and the humility to listen, no matter where your journey takes you.

Welcome to your newest resource for that extra arsenal of wisdom and proactive knowledge,

Unleashing Firepower, Masters of Business Excellence.

The gameboard is all set up, it is your move.

"Could Navy Seal Training Prepare You to Become a Better Entrepreneur?"

Jeff Engel

Jeff Engel has a diversified background that has spanned the Navy SEAL's, corporate world, and entrepreneurship.

During his time in the Navy SEAL's, Jeff worked alongside Special Forces units from various countries in the Middle East and Asia with a particular focus on operations in the Middle East.

Following his time in the military, Jeff went on to work for IBM and became an integral part of four startups. Jeff was also part of a small team that successfully grew a 15,000-person, $400 million company to a 31,000-person, $1.2 billion powerhouse in just ten years, which was eventually acquired as a strategic imperative.

Jeff attributes much of his success in the business world to his time in the Navy SEAL's working directly for people like Admiral McRaven.

Jeff would equate the SEAL's to improving his Grittiness, Hardiness, and Resilience while at the same time learning how to think through tactical decisions in a strategic way.

"Adversity reveals genius, prosperity conceals it."

HORACE

As a former US Navy SEAL, I had the opportunity to work with some of the "Best of the Best."

I am grateful and humbled to have realized that the combination of Grit, Perseverance, and Tenacity have been the critical ingredients needed to create a winning edge, that secret sauce between the battlefield and the boardroom.

One example of the "best of the best" is my former boss, William H. McRaven, who later became a four-star Admiral and the head of the Joint Special Operations Command.

Another was one of my platoon mates whose previous actions are under review for the Medal of Honor.

Still, another was a platoon mate who was one of the snipers in the Captain Phillips Hostage Rescue, and there are others whose accomplishments cannot be disclosed as they are still deemed confidential.

Each of these feats stands on its own as awe-inspiring. It was the work completed years before these accomplishments that enabled these feats to be successfully achieved.

Grit. Hardiness, Tenacity.

Many will say what is done in the US Navy SEAL's cannot truly be translated to the business world. Really?

To defend their point, they will attempt to highlight the selection process that weeds out 75% of candidates after they have already gone through an arduous initial selection process.

They will talk about 'Hell Week' which starts on Sunday and goes on until Friday where candidates are able to get about four hours of sleep during the period, a week that eliminates more than half the class.

They will also highlight the continuous training that SEAL's complete during their career including foreign languages and advanced education at top universities such as Harvard, MIT, and others.

My thought: It is exactly "that logic" that justifies why what is done in the SEAL's can indeed be translated transformatively into the business world.

It simply comes down to three rules and seven guiding principles.

1. Combine the right people (Talent on Teams).
2. Keep making the people better (Continuous Improvement/ Training).
3. Find the camaraderie that allows everyone to be Gritty, Hardy, and Tenacious (Leadership Culture).

Guiding Principles:

- Surround yourself with overachievers who are underestimated.
- Show up.
- Understand the process of the craft.
- Have open and constructive conversations.
- Plan, Execute, and Review.
- Everyone continuously learns.
- Consciously be Naive.

Surround yourself with overachievers who are underestimated

Surrounding yourself with overachievers who are underestimated starts with yourself. If you are not able to achieve things that others do not think are possible, how can you expect to attract others with these attributes to be part of your team? An overachiever who is underestimated is NOT the person who has been able to charm their way through situations.

Overachievers are the type of people who still deliver results even when people are not watching them. They are the men and women that when they hit the "figurative wall," they identify how to go over, under, around, or through. They are the people who when their attempts to overcome the "figurative wall" fail, their tenacity, grit, and hardiness push them to try again.

They simply get it done... No fanfare ... they just get it done. The true teammates like those I stood side by side with as a platoon commander at SEAL Team THREE or my teammates at Location Tech Inc., my current venture, persevere because they did not or do not want to let their teammates down.

Show up

Michael Jordan (Basketball), Koby Bryant (Basketball), Tom Brady (Football), and Kelly Slater (Surfer) were/are great in their respective endeavors. Each in his own right has been called the GOAT (Greatest of All Time). They were not always at the top, but what they all did was they "showed up" and put the work in to get better. They identified what they wanted to improve and put in the work to accomplish what they deemed appropriate for success. Often showing up means starting and ending before everyone else.

My teammates, not that I condone it and often I am in awe, work many weekends, and continuously late at night. I am also mindful that they are savvy enough to recognize that they need to sneak out during the day to show up for their kids' games and family occasions, giving back through volunteering events and other notable events. (Remember five years after the team separates, your family will still be there. Create memories for the people that matter long term.)

Understand the process of the craft

Sure, showing up is important, but great teammates understand the craft and their specialty within the larger craft/project/mission/statement of work. As a Navy SEAL, we spend countless hours week after week perfecting a certain skill and then switching to a different skill and practicing that. After honing each skill, everything is brought together in a manner that everyone understands the total craft and the sub-components of the craft. In the SEAL platoons, we also have department heads and assistant department heads who were accountable for that respective equipment. We had weapons, air, dive, First LT, Intel, and a couple of other areas. When we were given a task order, each department would prepare the gear to execute the task order.

The exact same process is done in the business world. Currently, within the team I am privileged to lead at my company, Location Tech, we have a person ultimately responsible for System Architecture, Software Development, Quality Assurance, Productive Development, Marketing, and Sales.

The same epiphany hits me every time I talk or think about my SEAL Platoons or Location Tech. It is the things that no one sees or acknowledges that pay dividends down the road.

By understanding your craft and your team understanding their craft well enough, everyone can plan for what is going to be needed 12 to 18 months from now; that is those things that are only known ahead of time because everyone understands their craft and what they uniquely need to bring to the team.

Have open and constructive conversations

Within my SEAL Platoons and today within Location Tech, we have continuous conversations about current and future things that need to be delivered.

It could be sales-related, marketing, or software/product-related.

While most conversations are great, move things along, and advance goals in a harmonious way, not all conversations are what we "want" to discuss.

I want to be noticeably clear that my point is not to speak to someone in an unkind manner under the guise of "straight talk," but rather to communicate in a way to help others understand that you disagree and why.

From there, it becomes a conversation of what needs to be addressed.

Priorities Matter.

Another valuable lesson I learned from one of my Assistant Officers in Charge (AOIC) in the SEAL Teams was to keep the "open conversation" within the confines of the group and not speak outside of the group.

Many times, taking the discussion outside is weaponizing it.

If the outside discussion can be considered gossip, condescending, and spoken outside the group, then your words inappropriately weaponized the conversation.

With open conversations, you need to be prepared to openly reflect in order to determine the honest answers to the following questions:

1. Are they right and you are wrong?
2. Is your concept right but not articulated in a meaningful/appropriate manner?
3. Is your logic right but completely off in every other manner?
4. Is your logic fundamentally wrong?
5. If the first four bullets do not fit during the self-reflection, why does the person believe what they do?
6. Is there a better solution that can come from the conversation?

Plan, Execute, and Review

A good team is composed of individuals who come together aligned with what they are working to achieve. They identify the task that needs to be accomplished. They create a plan. They execute the plan. After executing the plan, they review it to identify what worked and what can be done to improve the next time.

This is not magic.

It is rather a simple concept but extremely easy to slack off leading to the failure of executing each step in a meaningful manner. I would argue that most people think they can wing it and it will be okay.

Also Planning, Executing, and Reviewing do not need to be complex arduous processes.

Each discipline such as Sales, Marketing, Software, and Hardware development has different tools and processes to help effectively plan, execute, and review. These tools and processes are not one-size-fits-all. (Our head of product at Location Tech is really good at "reviewing"/listening which has helped move our product along to better serve our customers.)

Everyone continuously learns

While I would hope that this is intuitively obvious that we can always learn, overachievers who are underestimated realize that learning which can take many different forms is how one gets over, under, around, or through the "figurative wall" when previous attempts have failed. Continuous learning also helps a person prepare for something that he knows he will need to address 12 to 18 months down the road.

I have personally completed education programs through places like Columbia University (Finance), University of Illinois Urbana (Digital Marketing), Vayner Media course (Digital Marketing), and University of San Diego MBA with an emphasis in Supply Chain (to help me translate my military language to the words used in the business world).

All these programs and others were completed with a specific purpose to ensure I was able to contribute to the team more effectively than prior to starting the programs. Over the last few years, everyone within Location Tech has done something to improve the skills they bring to the Location Tech team.

Consciously be Naive

Doing tough things that others do not think are possible or worthy of effort requires you to be slightly naive. Kids are naturally curious about their parents. They joyfully ask their parents questions … Sometimes they will ask the question several times. But what they are doing as they are asking the question is learning and growing. While the parents may become frustrated, the kids naively press on and, in the process, grow.

It is this naivety that is sometimes needed to engage consciously to move through feats others would not dare to. In tough environments, you take someone's criticism and annoyance with you with a "grain of salt." With a grain of salt, there is probably a nugget within their words or thoughts; use those to help you think through the possibilities as you and the team drive to success.

My hope is that the very words that sustained me, "I believe in you," which enabled me to find the confidence required, will also enable you to realize that you really can achieve what you want to achieve.

Best of luck on your journey. Hooyah!

Coach MJ's Firepower takeaways from Jeff Engel

Embrace Grit, Perseverance, and Tenacity...

These qualities are invaluable for both the battlefield and the boardroom. They are the secret sauce for creating a winning edge. Embodying these attributes means you have the capacity to tackle significant challenges, push through failures, and stay committed until your goals are achieved.

Value of Team Dynamics and Continuous Growth:

- Right People and Camaraderie: Surround yourself with over-achievers who are underestimated. This ensures a team that will deliver results even when the odds are against them. Team members should have the resilience to face obstacles, displaying tenacity, grit, and hardiness. Cultivate a leadership culture that values and encourages these attributes.

- Continuous Learning and Improvement: Always strive to be better. Whether it's through formal education, as Jeff Engel did, or informal self-improvement, the best teams are always pushing their boundaries. This also implies understanding one's craft deeply, always showing up, and being proactive in planning, execution, and review.

Open and Constructive Conversations:

Foster an environment where team members can freely communicate their thoughts, even when they disagree. This ensures that everyone is on the same page and working towards a unified goal. However, it's vital to ensure these conversations remain constructive and within the team, avoiding gossip or external negativity.

Plan, Execute, Review:

This three-step approach is a foundational business strategy. Plan out your actions based on a solid understanding of your goals. Then, put those plans into action. After execution, always review what went right and what could be improved. This iterative process ensures continuous growth and refinement.

Harness the Power of Naivety: Being a little naive allows you to approach problems without the burden of perceived limitations. Just like a child's endless curiosity and persistence in asking questions, this naivety can drive innovation and encourage the tackling of challenges others might shy away from. Taking criticisms with a "grain of salt" and finding learning opportunities within them can lead to unexpected solutions and success.

Remember, the principles and attributes forged in the crucible of the toughest training environments, such as the SEAL's, can be unparalleled success transformative when applied to business.

Embrace them, and you're on a path to win...

Well Done, Jeff Engel!

"Mastering the Leadership Tango: Confidence, Competence, and Their Symbiotic Rhythms"

Dr. Bob Choat

Bob Choat, PhD, hosts The School of Transformation Podcast and authored "Mind Your Own Fitness" and the upcoming "Develop the Champion Within." He founded Mind Hack Academy and shares peak performance insights in various publications. Known as the Transformational Grandmaster, he's been featured on KABC TalkRadio, Cosozo Radio Network, Sirius Satellite Radio, and Hypnosis Today TV Show.

Bob, a Marine Veteran, and former LAPD Police Officer, holds a 5th-degree black belt in Kenpo, is a Jeet Kune Do Sr. Instructor, and a Close Quarter Combat Master Instructor. With one of his PhD's in psychology, he's an NLP-certified trainer, Executive Coach, and Peak Performance Mindset Master Trainer. In his free time, he enjoys Parkour and outdoor activities.

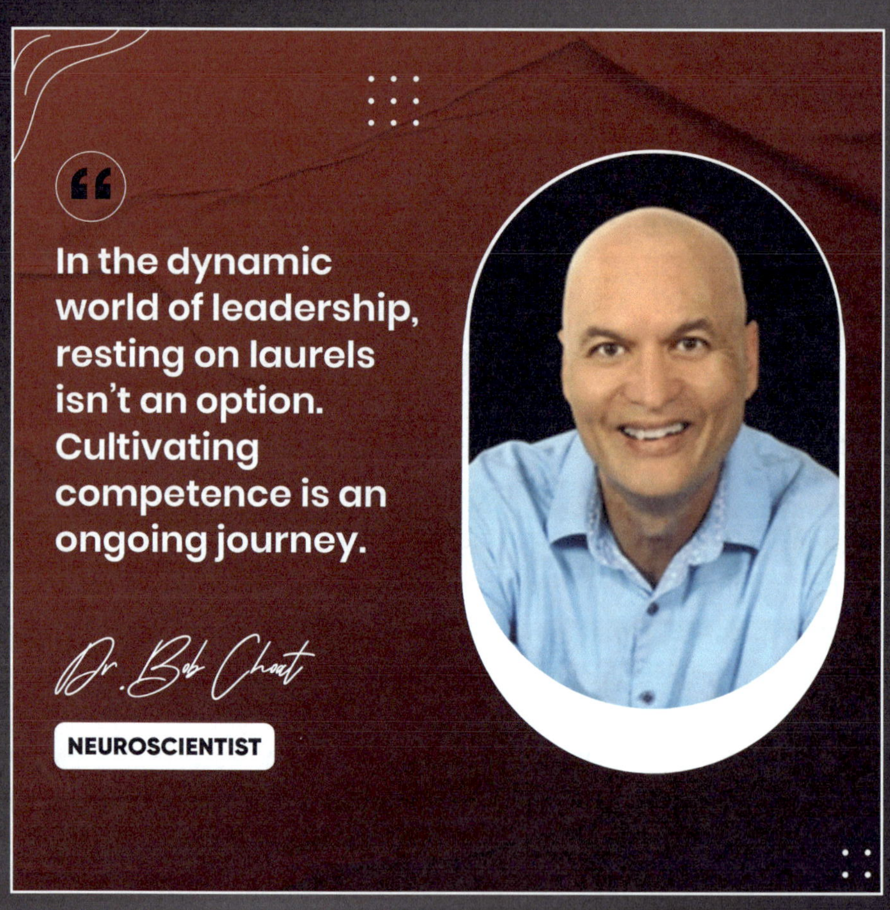

"Real knowledge is to know the extent of one's ignorance."

CONFUCIUS

Have you ever spotted a peacock in its full glory, spreading its dazzling feathers? Some leaders are like that peacock, flashing their confidence without the backbone of competence. While that confidence may be captivating, it is the true skill and know-how that sustains leadership.

Over the course of my life, I've seen leaders of every type. Some were good, some were bad, others were quite bad, and many were absolutely lousy and dangerous as leaders. The challenges facing leadership today and into the future will stem from whether or not those leaders are competent and will be able to deal with the many changes that happen.

Yet will it ever change regarding incompetence? As Dr. Laurence Peter stated in his famous book, The Peter Principle, "I have noticed that, with few exceptions, men bungle their affairs. Everywhere I see incompetence rampant, incompetence triumphant...I have accepted the universality of incompetence." He goes on further to explain, "In most hierarchies, super-competence is more objectionable than incompetence." This can be explained that many leaders fear those that are more competent than them and may even try to get rid of those competent people.

Table of Contents:

1. The Landscape of Overconfidence

The intriguing dance between leadership and confidence has long been the subject of many debates, discussions, and deep dives. It is like the sun;

essential in the right amount, but too much of it can cause a severe burn. There seems to be a rise in overconfidence among leaders today and even invited by many who falsely believe this is the key to a strong leader.

What Exactly Is Overconfidence?

In the simplest terms, overconfidence refers to an inflated view of one's abilities or knowledge. Picture this: someone driving into a storm, believing they can navigate it without any issues despite all warnings, only because they think they're the best driver out there. It is not about bravery or courage; it is an overestimation of one's abilities. I recall reading about an experienced US Army Ranger who was overconfident about his abilities to handle being swept away by a raging river that he refused help. His body was found later downstream.

Origins of Overconfidence in Leaders:

1. Early Successes: One success can sometimes create an illusion that every decision made will be right. It is like winning a gamble and believing you've cracked the code.
2. Yes-men Culture: When leaders surround themselves with individuals who only agree, it inflates their ego.
3. The Illusion of Control: Leaders often think they can control all variables. In reality, external factors like market dynamics, competition, and global events often play a more significant role than one imagines.

Why Overconfidence Can Be Dangerous:

- Blind Spots: Overconfident leaders often fail to recognize the potential pitfalls in their strategies. Like driving with tinted glasses at night, they're unable to see the dangers lurking in the shadows.

- Resistance to Feedback: Confidence can sometimes morph into arrogance. When that happens, genuine feedback, even if it is for the betterment of the organization, gets ignored or worse, ridiculed.
- Risk Taking: While taking risks is an inherent part of leadership, overconfident leaders tend to take unnecessary risks, putting their teams and organizations in jeopardy.

Spotting Overconfidence:

It is essential, both for leaders and their teams, to identify overconfidence and differentiate it from genuine confidence. Some signs include:

- Dismissing others' opinions without consideration.
- Never admitting mistakes or deflecting blame onto others.
- Always needing to have the final word or dominate conversations.

Remember the peacock metaphor? Overconfident leaders might be showy and eye-catching, but if their display isn't backed by the strength of competence, the dazzle quickly fades to reveal a lack of substance. Think about the boisterous and charismatic leader who exclaims that he knows it all and that only he can make things happen.

Combating Overconfidence:

If you're a leader, it is crucial to keep a check on your confidence levels. Engage in:

- Self-reflection and Self-Awareness: Regular introspection can help one understand their strengths and weaknesses. Knowing thyself is a real key to becoming a good leader.
- 360-degree feedback: This is where employees at all levels give feedback, providing a holistic view of a leader's effectiveness.

- Continued Learning: Remember, the landscape of business and leadership continually evolves. Being a lifelong learner ensures you're always prepared.

In a nutshell, while confidence is an integral aspect of leadership, it becomes a double-edged sword when not balanced with competence and self-awareness.

2. The Pitfalls of Incompetence: A Dive into Historical Blunders

History isn't just a collection of dates and events. It is a teacher, showcasing patterns of human behavior and the resultant consequences. While tales of great leadership and visionaries are inspirational, tales of blunders made due to overconfidence and incompetence serve as cautionary reminders.

Defining Incompetence in Leadership:

At its core, incompetence is the inability to perform required tasks, make informed decisions, or lead effectively. It is not just about lacking skills or knowledge but also about the failure to realize and rectify these deficiencies.

Historical Blunders Stemming from Overconfidence and Incompetence:

- The Sinking of the Titanic (1912): A tragic example where overconfidence in technology and underestimation of nature led to the loss of more than 1,500 lives. Despite receiving multiple iceberg warnings, Captain Edward Smith continued at full speed. The ship was deemed "unsinkable," which fostered a false sense of security.

- The Bay of Pigs Invasion (1961): A failed attempt by U.S.-trained Cuban exiles to invade Cuba and overthrow Fidel Castro. The operation, underestimating the Cuban forces and overestimating local support, turned out to be a significant blunder, severely embarrassing the Kennedy administration.
- The Charge of the Light Brigade (1854): During the Crimean War, miscommunication and overconfidence led British cavalry forces into a frontal assault against well-defended Russian artillery. The result? Heavy casualties and a lesson on the importance of clear communication and competent decision-making.

Consequences of Incompetence:

- Lost Lives and Resources: As seen with the Titanic and Charge of the Light Brigade, incompetent leadership doesn't just risk material or financial loss but also precious human lives.
- Damaged Reputation: Failures, especially those stemming from clear incompetence, can tarnish reputations for decades, if not longer. The aftermath of the Bay of Pigs is still discussed in political circles.
- Lost Opportunities: While not as glaring as other consequences, missed chances due to incompetence can change the course of history. Opportunities, once gone, might never return.

Learning from Historical Incompetence:

One might wonder: Why study these blunders? It is not about finger-pointing but understanding and internalizing.

- Acknowledging Limitations: Accepting that one might not have all the answers is the first step towards avoiding incompetence.

- Valuing Expertise: Just as Captain Smith should have heeded iceberg warnings; leaders should respect and listen to experts in pertinent fields.
- Preparing for the Unforeseen: The Titanic tragedy could have been lessened with enough lifeboats. Preparing for worst-case scenarios, even if they seem unlikely, is crucial.

In the grand tapestry of history, instances of incompetence serve as stark, often tragic reminders of the weight and responsibility leadership holds. It underscores the vital importance of pairing confidence with competence, and vision with vigilance.

3. Power of True Competence

While the siren song of overconfidence can lure many, the steadfast and humble beacon of true competence offers guidance, strength, and the promise of genuine accomplishment. True competence is the foundation on which successful leadership is built, ensuring that confidence is not merely a facade but substantiated by skill, knowledge, and experience.

What Is True Competence?

It is not just about being good at what you do. It is about being adept, constantly improving, and understanding the dynamics of the ever-changing world around you. It is the fusion of skill, knowledge, experience, and adaptability. I'm always challenging myself to grow as a person and as a leader. I realize that I can only do this by becoming more and more competent.

Key Attributes of Competent Leaders:

1. Knowledge Mastery: Competent leaders are well-versed in their respective domains. They stay updated with the latest trends, research, and methodologies. They're not just jack-of-all-trades, but masters of their realm.
2. Adaptability: The ability to pivot and recalibrate strategies in response to changes is a hallmark of competence. They don't flounder when faced with the unexpected; they adapt.
3. Empathy: Beyond just professional expertise, competent leaders understand the human element. They connect with their teams, fostering environments of mutual respect and understanding.

Why True Competence Matters:

- Long-term Vision: While overconfidence might offer short-lived victories, true competence shapes a vision that stands the test of time and challenges.
- Trust and Credibility: Competence breed's trust. Teams are more inclined to follow, and stakeholders are more likely to invest when they see a leader with a proven track record and clear expertise.
- Risk Management: Competent leaders can better gauge risks, understand potential pitfalls, and design strategies to mitigate them.

Building and Nurturing Competence:

In the dynamic world of leadership, resting on laurels isn't an option. Cultivating competence is an ongoing journey.

- Continuous Learning: From workshops to courses, books to seminars – staying updated is paramount.

- Mentorship: Engaging with mentors, those who have "been there, done that," provides invaluable insights and perspectives.
- Feedback Reception: Openness to feedback, even if it is critical, paves the way for growth and improved competence.

Dr. John Maxwell's words, "Leaders become great, not because of their power, but because of their ability to empower others," ring especially true here. It is not just about personal competence but fostering an environment where everyone is empowered to be competent, to grow, learn, and flourish.

True competence is the heart and soul of leadership. It is the engine that drives the vision, the compass that guides through challenges, and the foundation that ensures sustained success. While the shimmer of overconfidence might be tempting, the steady, resilient glow of competence is what truly illuminates the path of exemplary leadership.

4. Unraveling the Spiral: The Competence-Confidence Loop in Leadership Dynamics

1. The Positive Loop:

a. Initial Competence: Let's say you acquire a new skill, like playing the guitar. At first, you might not be incredibly good at it, but with practice, you become more competent.
b. Increased Confidence: As you notice improvement in your guitar-playing abilities, your belief in your ability to play the guitar grows. This newfound confidence motivates you to play in front of friends or even perform at a local event.
c. Pursuit of Further Competence: Emboldened by your boosted confidence, you might decide to take advanced guitar lessons or practice more regularly, further enhancing your competence.

d. Confidence Grows Again: With even more skills under your belt, your confidence increases further, continuing the positive cycle.

2. The Negative Loop:

a. Lack of Competence: On the flip side, if you try something new and find it challenging without seeing any immediate improvement, you might feel you lack competence.
b. Decreased Confidence: Feeling you're not good at the task can reduce your confidence, making you less likely to engage in it or practice.
c. Avoidance of Skill Development: Due to diminished confidence, you might avoid the activity altogether, missing out on opportunities to build competence.
d. Confidence Drops Further: As you continually avoid the task, your confidence in that area deteriorates even more, perpetuating the negative cycle.

Breaking/Maintaining the Loop:

- For the Positive Loop: It is essential to keep challenging oneself and seeking opportunities for growth. Complacency can halt the loop. Celebrate small victories, seek feedback, and always remain a learner.
- For the Negative Loop: The key is intervention. Recognize the declining confidence and take proactive steps. This could mean seeking mentorship, practicing more, breaking tasks into manageable steps, or reframing failures as learning opportunities.

In essence, the competence-confidence loop underscores the interconnectedness of our beliefs in our abilities and our actual skills. The relationship between the two can be a powerful driver of personal and professional growth or, if not recognized and managed, a barrier to progress.

5. The Inseparable Dance of Confidence and Competence

The relationship between confidence and competence can be likened to that of the sun and the moon. Both are celestial bodies that illuminate our world, but their brilliance and purpose differ vastly. While one might shine brighter at times, it is the harmonious dance of these two that brings balance to our days and nights.

Understanding the Dance:

To appreciate the beauty of this dance, it is crucial to understand the intrinsic value of both confidence and competence.

1. Confidence: It is self-belief that propels leaders to take the initiative, make decisions, and lead from the front. It is the driving force, the momentum that ignites action.
2. Competence: This is the expertise, the knowledge, the skill set. It is the substance behind the action, ensuring the steps taken aren't just bold but also informed and wise.

Why This Dance Matters:

- Empowerment: A balance of confidence and competence allows leaders to empower not only themselves but their teams. It breeds a culture of informed action and fearless pursuit of objectives.
- Trust Building: Stakeholders, teams, or clients are more likely to trust a leader who exudes confidence backed by demonstrable competence.

- Sustainable Success: While confidence might kickstart projects, it is competence that ensures their completion and long-term success.

Pitfalls of a Lopsided Dance:

Imagine a dance where one partner overshadows the other, or worse, steps on the other's toes.

- Overconfidence without Competence: This often leads to hasty decisions, unchecked risks, and an inability to see potential pitfalls. It is like driving fast in the fog with headlights off.
- Competence without Confidence: Here, despite having the skills and knowledge, leaders might hesitate to take initiative, voice opinions, or make crucial decisions. It is akin to owning a sports car but being too scared to drive it.

Nurturing the Balance:

So, how does one ensure this dance remains harmonious?

- Self-awareness: Leaders need to frequently introspect, evaluate their confidence levels, and ensure they align with their actual skills and knowledge.
- Continued Learning: Ensuring that one's confidence is always backed by updated competence is crucial. As Albert Einstein wisely put it, "Once you stop learning, you start dying."
- Seeking Feedback: This provides an external perspective, helping leaders understand if their confidence is perceived as arrogance or if their competence is being effectively communicated and utilized.

To wrap up, the dance of confidence and competence is intricate but integral. Leaders must strive to keep these forces in harmony, ensuring neither overshadows the other. For in their balance lies the secret to transformative leadership that leaves an indelible mark on history.

"Everybody's got a different circle of competence. The important thing is not how big the circle is. The important thing is staying inside the circle." – Warren Buffett

Coach MJ's Firepower Takeaways from Dr. Bob Choat

The Double-Edged Sword of Confidence:

- Overconfidence vs. True Confidence: Leaders need to be wary of the trap of overconfidence which can blind them to risks and potential pitfalls. Overconfidence stems from early successes, a culture of "yes-men", and illusions of control. Genuine confidence, on the other hand, is backed by competence and self-awareness.

- Spotting & Combating Overconfidence: Leaders should be alert to signs like dismissing others' opinions, not admitting mistakes, and dominating conversations. Self-reflection, 360-degree feedback, and continuous learning can keep overconfidence in check.

Recognizing limitations, valuing expertise, and preparing for unforeseen challenges can prevent such blunders.

The Powerhouse of True Competence:

- Defining Competence: It goes beyond being skilled. It's about mastery, adaptability, and a deep connection with teams. True competence is being adept, continuously improving, and staying relevant.

- Cultivating Competence: Continuous learning, seeking mentorship, and being receptive to feedback are pivotal. As Dr. John Maxwell aptly noted, great leaders empower others, and empowerment stems from competence.

Incorporating these critical insights into leadership practices can steer leaders towards informed, competent, and genuinely confident leadership, leaving a lasting and positive impact.

Thank you, Dr. Bob Choat!

"You Are Remarkable Because You Are Resilient. Believe It."

Christina Dodd

Christina is an executive coach, corporate trainer, and facilitator in leadership transformation, emotional intelligence, and life and business skills growth.

She is a seasoned business owner, mentor, and HR consultant with over 25 years' experience. Her expertise in the field of human development and achievement comes armed with a career in government, advertising, executive search, MLM, training and development, and educating entrepreneurs to grow their own businesses.

Christina is an Australian citizen who has also lived and worked in Southeast Asia for over 30 years. Her clients are based in Vietnam, Malaysia, and the Southeast Asia region.

Her reach includes France (Europe), the UAE, KSA, and Morocco (MENA).

"Let yourself be silently drawn by the strange pull of what you really love. It will not lead you astray."

RUMI.

Within each of us – within you – there is an instinctive, urging and almost profound ability that enables us when confronted to tap into our strengths, to work through challenging experiences in order to bounce back, and to move forward.

It is such an empowering capability and force that it can change our circumstances, change our world, and change our lives for the better. In times of all manner of hurt and struggle and the most daunting challenges that face us and which reappear with increased ferocity, just when we thought we had dealt with them, we rise up, and we adapt and go full-on into tackling that which has dared to defy and confront us.

We find the stamina – somehow and some way – to pick ourselves up out of the deep dark hole that just swallowed us and keep going!

My heart is pounding as I write this because this is exactly what this book is all about.

Unleashing Firepower Masters of Business Excellence is here to uplift you, to fuel that fire within you so that you can become more resilient and excel.

Its purpose is to eliminate any doubt in your mind that you have this extraordinary capability, which when unleashed, enables you to work magic.

This book is a priceless gift to you from my incredible colleague and friend, Coach MJ Tolan, who is living proof of the power of resilience.

The contents will encourage and build within you the confidence to overcome, to manage, and to survive all that challenges you; to find the courage to persevere and to shine with optimism; and to inspire you to keep looking ever-forward.

You will find the ability to rise above your personal hardship; to harness the uniqueness that is beautifully you and to build on that; to strengthen your strengths; to see that there are possibilities ahead of you, despite what you're going through in life or in business.

I am honored to be a part of this noble journey with Michael and the other like-minded driven colleagues gathered here to set you on an upward course of action.

We hope to elevate you to reach the pinnacle of your corporate career; to become that successful business owner or aspire to be; to become a valued and respected leader in your community; or to be of service to something "bigger" in your life.

I am here to share my experiences with you, and I hope that our pathways will connect so that I can help you to become more resilient, more confident, and more knowledgeable about what you need to do and how, so you can achieve those things that are most important to you in your world.

It would be my privilege to guide and encourage you on this journey. I have always loved being around people.

People fascinate me and human behavior even more so. Why we do the things we do is a never-ending study of mine.

I am thrilled that it is my passion and my chosen field of business and life's work. I never tire of listening because everyone has a story to tell, and I am interested.

I enjoy sharing my thoughts and my words with others so that I may enlighten them and lift them up.

That is me. I gave my very first speech at my high school when I was 15 years old.

I had just returned from an exciting year of schooling in Malaysia where my father had been posted with the Royal Australian Airforce.

I came back to Australia to further my studies.

My parents remained there for several years. It was a tender time, but I wouldn't change it for the world.

I remember feeling nervous standing on the stage but strangely comfortable and at ease even though the hall was filled with hundreds of noisy and somewhat disinterested chatterboxes.

When it was my turn to speak, they suddenly stopped. They hadn't seen me for a year and were eager to know what I was going to say.

I related several experiences of living overseas, the culture, and the strange and exotic things I had seen. They sat poised, listening intently. Some of the more hilarious situations I recounted left them rolling in their seats along with some of the very conservative faculty.

It felt good to connect with my colleagues and teachers. I felt good, and it was exhilarating. I knew from then on that I was destined for a career which revolved around people and humanity.

I realized at that young age that I had a deep sense of appreciation for others, that I liked seeing people enthusiastic and enjoying themselves, and that I had a way to reach them. I knew that I wanted to give so much more.

The Spark that Fueled my Passion and Brought Me to Where I Am.

I answered a small ad in a local newspaper in Bangkok. It was as simple as that. It read, "Speakers needed to help business owners become winners.

No experience required. Training provided." I was intrigued, and I started to visualize my future and what it could look like. My imagination ran wild. I should tell you that I first relocated to Bangkok in 1984 from Australia with an energetic and adventurous spirit (and husband), and we simply stayed. I worked for various companies there and in the region, including Vietnam, for many years.

You might say Southeast Asia was and still is my backyard, where I have spent a great part of my adult life and where I currently base myself whilst exploring the rest of the world, of course – the possibilities are endless!

Anyway, back to the ad. At that time in 1997, I was feeling burnt-out and despondent, dissatisfied with the job I held in a head-hunting firm because things weren't buzzing for me.

I was in a people-industry which I enjoyed, but I began to feel too constrained and felt I was just a part of some huge piece of machinery. I wanted something new and different, something inspiring where I could connect on a different and perhaps deeper level with people. It was time for me to make that leap. So, I answered the ad and got an interview. I was thrilled. I prepared myself for the standard interview routine.

Well, what a surprise! What eventuated was something entirely unexpected. Never had I met such energetic and encouraging people who weren't really interested in my qualifications or work history, but who were more engrossed in me, my desires, my experiences, why I enjoyed being around people and how I could inspire them to achieve their dreams.

I thought, where have these people been all my life?

I like this. No, I love this! That's when the penny dropped for me. I had finally found what I was looking for. The people I met were driven with an ambition that I had not witnessed in any company I had previously worked for. I suddenly became more alive.

This was my entry into the world of MLM, and I had no idea what I was in for. Nothing prepared me for the time ahead. It was vibrant and all-empowering, life-changing, and it took me throughout Southeast Asia to the U.S. and one to one of the most rewarding times of my career and my life. Being surrounded by all positivity, grounded in throbbing wholesome intention, is what inflamed my passion. From the very moment I joined this new world, I began to grow as a person, and I could literally feel it happening.

The training was phenomenal and filled with truths and wisdom about who we are and what makes us tick. I loved it and took to it like a duck to water.

I was a natural on stage and delivered seminars all from memory and from my heart. I read more books than I had ever read before, learned about humanness and entrepreneurship, and how to win in business and in life, how to let go, and how to overcome.

I met and talked with, celebrated, and hugged thousands of people from all walks of life and discovered who I am, and what is precious and important to me. I discovered the power of the individual, of human achievement.

I discovered my power and my calling. What inspired me and touched me the most during this entire experience was the way every single human being was treated. People mattered, and this resonated deeply with me.

This milestone in my life compelled me to start my own training and development company which over the years has become a consultancy. It is through this niche entity that we develop the human, the essential, and the life and professional skills every individual needs to thrive and prosper on a personal level and in their chosen career.

We enable small businesses and organizations to succeed through developing their most precious asset – their people – building a leadership brimming with outstanding human leaders. What I have learned through my experience over the years in motivational training, which I loyally guard and cherish, is foundational to how I work with my clients.

I coach and guide and empower every individual driven by my pure and genuine concern for their well-being because they are worth every ounce of my effort and deserve the success they are looking for. I very strongly believe that everyone – that you – can excel in life, or in whatever you desire to do or to be, if only given the opportunity to be heard, to be coached, and to be encouraged along the way.

You Will Excel and You Will Achieve. Your EI Will Make Sure of It.

It isn't easy, let's be honest, to run your own business or any company for that matter and to succeed. I admire anyone who has the gumption and a real die-hard attitude to begin a start-up. That's a real roller coaster ride. The higher you climb the executive ladder, and the more you go all out to be your own boss to make a million dollars from that product or service you created, the longer and more complex your days – and nights – become. Stress is ever-present and in abundance.

Anyone with people to manage or lead has a challenging task ahead of them without a doubt. The key to thriving and surviving at the top, and, in fact, getting there is having a learning and growth mindset. Without this, you may as well close up shop! I'm not only referring here to the nuts-and-bolts knowledge, the hardware or the hard skills required of you in your business or your job, or the new innovations in your product line, AI (Artificial Intelligence), or market trends and the like.

I'm referring to your knowledge of you, of yourself and of you having a learning and growth mindset and a genuine willingness to continue to develop yourself.

This means developing your emotional intelligence to the level where you can navigate your way successfully through all that throws itself in your path and all that is your responsibility. You have come to this point for which you deserve oceans of applause, but there are still things you need to learn and to know and to improve upon.

You can always be better at what you do and how you conduct yourself. I have a feeling you totally agree with me.

You can and will excel and achieve… because your EI will make sure you do. That resilience within you… it comes under the umbrella of EI and how you identify, understand, and manage your emotions.

Together, they carry you onward and upward. In all my years of experience and from credible research on the subject, the neediest of all when it comes to emotional intelligence are the senior-level executives.

I'm also referring to the C-suite here and, of course, anyone who is a business owner. Being in this position can be empowering and rewarding, and at the same time it can also be a nightmare, debilitating, loaded with stress and expectation, and full of burn-out and despair.

To stay the distance and be exceptional and on top of the game – is a major feat. I have the deepest respect for anyone at these levels because it is not always sunshine and roses.

Being in important and powerful positions is a lot of hard work although sometimes the rank and file may not think so. Being at the top demands so much of a person that unless you are up there, you really cannot comprehend just what that involves.

I know that you know… exactly what I'm talking about.

When I meet executives, just like you, I take the time to look into their eyes.

To see behind the facial expressions and the mask that is worn so frequently, so desperately in some cases.

For underneath all the facade is a person, a human being whom for whatever reason is calling out for some relief; for something or someone to hold on to before he/she loses it completely; for reassurance, for encouragement, for guidance because he/she really does not have all the answers like others think he/she does or expects.

The first response when I coach at this level is usually a huge sigh of relief.

The air is almost palpable with a release of emotions so hidden and intertwined with others, so buried, that it is clear to see how things became heavy and taxing. Businesses today and the corporate minefield we tread are fraught with intrusion and disruption.

This is partly due to the recent past and the pandemic and to the galloping speed at which AI is integrating itself into almost every facet of industry and life.

People are changing as the world is changing and so, too, is the baggage that we all carry.

This is precisely why each human being at the senior executive level, those who steer organizations towards the future, need to be open to learning more about themselves, to going deeper into accepting, caring for, and loving themselves.

They must become more adept at knowing and managing themselves well, so they may excel at knowing and managing others and all that it entails.

I feel that you understand this; that you get it as you most likely are re-counting your own experiences while reading this.

Developing your emotional intelligence and becoming emotionally literate and agile are no longer touchy subjects.

They are absolute necessities in life and business, in government and industry, and in service and community. It is critical to the way we conduct business and to the way we lead… today and beyond. For those I know and have coached and worked together on EI-related and leadership issues, they have gone from strength to strength. They have been renewed, revitalized, and reborn and although still confronted by never-ending challenges, have become increasingly capable of handling them and themselves responsibly and in an emotionally intelligent way. At the same time as reaching higher levels of performance, they have compounded their level of resilience, enabling them to take major strides forward. As I stated at the beginning of this chapter, You Are Remarkable Because You Are Resilient. Believe It. You have so much to offer your world, and once you can harness that resilience inside you and help it work its magic, you will achieve all that you are looking for and so much more. I simply cannot wait to meet you.

Coach MJ's Firepower Takeaways

Embrace Your Innate Resilience: Every individual possesses a powerful ability to confront challenges, adapt to situations, and bounce back from adversities.

The Power of Emotional Intelligence (EI): Emotional Intelligence is pivotal, especially for those in leadership and executive positions.

Always Maintain a Growth Mindset: Adopting a growth mindset, where you constantly seek to learn and evolve, is the cornerstone of success.

Human Connection & Authentic Leadership: Behind every executive title and corporate façade is a human being with emotions, aspirations, and vulnerabilities.

Embracing Challenges as Growth Opportunities: Life and business will always be replete with disruptions and challenges.

Applying these golden nuggets can instill a renewed sense of purpose, drive, and determination in individuals, helping them excel in their business ventures and personal journeys.

Very Insightful, Christina Dodd!

"The Power of Emotional Intelligence in Enhancing Customer Experience and Driving Business Growth"

Christopher Salem

Chris Salem is an accomplished CEO, Business Growth Strategist, Professional Keynote Speaker, Award-Winning Author, Business Trainer, Radio Show Host & Media Personality dedicated to empowering business owners' businesses to boost their brands and business simultaneously from ordinary to extraordinary.

His goal is straightforward – to help serious business owners foster better workplace environments that lead to higher engagement and retention with staff while generating more clients, increasing customer experiences, and scaling their overall revenue and profits quickly and inexpensively.

His book Master Your Inner Critic / Resolve the Root Cause – Create Prosperity became an international bestseller in 2016. He also co-authored the recent edition to "Mastering the Art of Success" with Jack Canfield. His weekly radio shows, Sustainable Success is part of the Voice America Business Channel and Business Influencers with TALRadio, part of the Touch-A-Life foundation.

"No act of kindness, no matter how small, is ever wasted."

AESOP

In today's rapidly evolving business landscape, emotional intelligence (EI) has emerged as a critical factor in shaping the success of a company.

Companies that are seriously exploring more sustainable methodologies to grow their business should strongly consider (EI) moving forward.

Let's delve into the profound impact of emotional intelligence on the customer experience and outline strategies to harness its potential for enhancing revenue and net profit.

Understanding Emotional Intelligence:

Emotional intelligence refers to the ability to recognize, understand, manage, and effectively use emotions in oneself and others. In the context of customer experience, EI plays a pivotal role in building strong relationships, fostering empathy, and creating memorable interactions.

When employees possess high levels of emotional intelligence, they can connect with customers on a deeper level, leading to increased satisfaction and loyalty.

What are the Components of Emotional Intelligence? Emotional intelligence is often broken down into five key components:

Self-awareness: This is the foundation of emotional intelligence.

Self-aware individuals understand their emotions, strengths, and weaknesses and how their feelings impact their thoughts and actions.

Self-regulation: This is the ability to manage and control one's emotions, even in challenging situations. This includes avoiding impulsive actions driven solely by emotions and maintaining a sense of balance. Motivation: People with high emotional intelligence are driven by a genuine passion for their goals rather than external rewards. They are resilient in the face of setbacks and remain focused on their objectives.

Empathy: Empathy involves recognizing and understanding the emotions of others. It allows individuals to connect on a deeper level, forming stronger relationships and fostering cooperation.

Social skills: Effective interpersonal skills are vital for navigating social situations. Those with high EQ excel in communication, conflict resolution, and teamwork, making them adept leaders and collaborators.

The Significance of Emotional Intelligence: Emotional intelligence plays a pivotal role in personal and professional success.

In personal relationships, individuals with high EQ are better equipped to understand their own requirements and the requirements of others, leading to healthier interactions and more fulfilling connections. In the workplace, emotional intelligence is a sought-after trait.

Leaders who possess high EQ tend to be more approachable, understanding, and inspiring.

They can motivate their teams, manage conflicts constructively, and adapt to changing situations with ease.

Moreover, employees with strong emotional intelligence contribute positively to team dynamics and are better at handling stress and pressure.

How Do You Cultivate Emotional Intelligence?

The good news is that emotional intelligence can be developed and refined over time.

Various strategies and practices can aid in the growth of EQ, such as self-reflection, mindfulness, active listening, and seeking feedback from others.

Engaging in these activities fosters greater self-awareness and a deeper understanding of emotions. Emotional intelligence is a multifaceted skill that goes beyond simply recognizing emotions—it involves understanding, managing, and effectively using them to navigate life's challenges.

By honing emotional intelligence, individuals can lead more fulfilling lives, build stronger relationships, and excel in both personal and professional spheres.

As we move forward, the importance of EQ continues to gain recognition, emphasizing its status as a fundamental aspect of human interaction and growth.

The Role of Emotional Intelligence in Customer Experience: In an increasingly competitive business landscape, delivering exceptional customer experiences has become a critical differentiator.

One of the key elements that significantly will influence customer interactions is emotional intelligence (EQ).

Let's explore how emotional intelligence plays a pivotal role in shaping customer experiences and building lasting relationships.

Empathetic Customer Interactions:

Employees with high EI are more attuned to customers' emotions and needs. They can respond empathetically to customer concerns, leading to a sense of understanding and trust.

Effective Conflict Resolution: EI empowers employees to handle conflicts and difficult situations with grace and empathy.

This skill is crucial for maintaining positive customer interactions and resolving issues satisfactorily.

Personalized Experiences: Emotional intelligence enables employees to personalize interactions based on customers' emotional states and preferences.

This personalized touch enhances the overall customer experience. In an era where customer loyalty and advocacy are crucial, emotional intelligence emerges as a pivotal factor in shaping memorable and positive customer experiences.

By recognizing and responding to customers' emotions, businesses can create deeper connections, build brand loyalty, and stand out in a crowded market. Incorporating emotional intelligence into customer interactions is not just a strategy; it is a testament to a brand's commitment to understanding and prioritizing the human aspect of business relationships.

Strategies for Leveraging Emotional Intelligence to Drive Revenue and Net Profit:

Emotional intelligence (EQ) has the power to transform not only personal interactions but also business outcomes.

Let's explore strategies that demonstrate how harnessing emotional intelligence can drive revenue growth and increase net profit, making it a valuable asset in the business world.

EI Training and Development: Implement comprehensive EI training programs for employees at all levels.

These programs can enhance emotional awareness, communication skills, and conflict-resolution abilities.

Hiring for Emotional Intelligence: During the recruitment process, prioritize candidates with strong EI traits.

Assessing emotional intelligence during hiring can lead to a workforce that is naturally inclined toward delivering exceptional customer experiences.

Reducing Employee Turnover and Costs: High employee turnover can be costly for businesses. Emotionally intelligent leaders create a supportive and empathetic work environment that boosts employee morale and job satisfaction.

This reduces turnover, minimizing recruitment and training costs. Happy employees are more productive and provide better customer service, positively impacting overall revenue.

Enhancing Marketing Strategies: Emotional intelligence can guide marketing strategies by helping companies tap into customers' emotional drives.

Ads and campaigns that evoke positive emotions are more likely to resonate with audiences and drive conversions. Emotional intelligence also aids in crafting authentic brand stories that connect with consumers, fostering brand loyalty and increasing market share.

Effective Leadership and Team Collaboration: Leaders with strong emotional intelligence can foster a positive work environment that encourages collaboration and innovation.

Emotionally intelligent leaders understand the motivations and concerns of their team members, leading to higher engagement and productivity.

This, in turn, translates to more efficient operations, higher-quality outputs, and increased profitability.

Feedback and Continuous Improvement:

Foster a culture of open feedback and continuous improvement. Encourage employees to share their insights on customer interactions and collaborate on refining strategies to enhance emotional intelligence in customer engagement.

Data-Driven Insights: Utilize data analytics to gain insights into customer emotions, preferences, and behavior. By analyzing this data, businesses can tailor their approaches and offerings to align with customer emotional needs.

Emotional Branding: Develop an emotional connection between customers and your brand.

Craft compelling narratives and marketing messages that resonate with customers on an emotional level, creating lasting brand loyalty.

Employee Wellbeing: Prioritize the emotional wellbeing of your employees.

A supportive work environment that values emotional health can lead to happier, more engaged employees who, in turn, provide better customer experiences.

Again, emotional intelligence is not only a tool for fostering better relationships—it is also a strategic asset for driving revenue growth and increasing net profit.

By understanding and responding to the emotions of customers, employees, and stakeholders, businesses can create a competitive edge that resonates in the bottom line.

Integrating emotional intelligence into various facets of the business landscape is a testament to its transformative power in enhancing both financial success and overall organizational well-being.

Measuring Success and Outcomes: In the modern business landscape, success is no longer solely measured by financial metrics.

Emotional intelligence (EQ) has emerged as a critical factor in determining the effectiveness and impact of business initiatives.

Let's delve into the methods and metrics used to measure success and outcomes in business by considering the influence of emotional intelligence.

Traditionally, success in business was often equated with profit margins and market share. However, this narrow focus is evolving to encompass a more holistic understanding of success—one that takes into account factors such as employee satisfaction, customer loyalty, brand reputation, and social impact. Emotional intelligence plays a pivotal role in shaping these dimensions of success.

Key Metrics for Measuring Emotional Intelligence-Driven Success

Employee Engagement: A workforce with high emotional intelligence is more engaged, motivated, and productive.

Measuring metrics such as employee satisfaction, retention rates, and collaboration levels can provide insights into the impact of emotional intelligence on organizational success.

Customer Loyalty and Satisfaction: Emotional intelligence influences how companies engage with customers on a personal level.

Metrics like Net Promoter Score (NPS), customer retention rates, and repeat business can reflect the positive outcomes of emotionally intelligent customer interactions.

Leadership Effectiveness: Emotionally intelligent leaders inspire and guide their teams more effectively.

Metrics such as leadership development programs' effectiveness, employee feedback on leadership, and team performance can shed light on the role of EQ in leadership success.

Brand Reputation and Trust: Emotional intelligence influences how a brand is perceived by its stakeholders.

Monitoring metrics like brand sentiment analysis, social media engagement, and customer testimonials can provide insights into emotional intelligence's impact on brand reputation.

Conflict Resolution and Communication: The ability to manage conflicts and communicate effectively is enhanced by emotional intelligence.

Reduced employee disputes improved cross-functional collaboration, and smoother internal communication are indicators of EQ-driven success.

Innovation and Adaptability: Emotionally intelligent organizations are better equipped to adapt to change and foster innovation.

Metrics such as idea generation, successful implementation of new strategies, and employee contributions to process improvement can reflect the role of EQ in innovation.

To gauge the impact of emotional intelligence on customer experience and business growth, consider the following metrics:

Customer Satisfaction Scores (CSAT): Track improvements in CSAT scores as emotional intelligence initiatives are implemented.

Customer Retention Rate: Monitor the rate at which customers return for repeat business, a key indicator of strong emotional connections.

Net Promoter Score (NPS): Evaluate the willingness of customers to recommend your business, reflecting their emotional attachment to your brand.

Revenue Growth: Analyze revenue trends over time and correlate them with emotional intelligence initiatives.

Employee Engagement: Measure improvements in employee engagement levels as emotional intelligence becomes an integral part of the company culture.

The Evolving Role of Emotional Intelligence in Business Success: Emotional intelligence is no longer an abstract concept; it has become a measurable and impactful driver of business success.

As companies continue to acknowledge the importance of EQ, it will play an increasingly integral role in shaping strategic decisions, fostering meaningful relationships, and achieving both financial and non-financial objectives. By incorporating emotional intelligence metrics into their assessment frameworks, businesses can ensure a more comprehensive understanding of success—one that encompasses the emotional and human aspects that truly drive positive outcomes. Overall, emotional intelligence is a powerful driver of enhanced customer experiences, leading to increased revenue and net profit. By cultivating emotional intelligence within the organization and aligning strategies to leverage its potential, businesses can foster lasting customer relationships and position themselves for sustained growth in the competitive marketplace. So, what are the next steps for your business to take your customer experience to the next level while increasing your revenue and net profit? Choosing to combine (EI) into your strategy can make all the difference in the long term with more successful outcomes.

Coach MJ's Firepower Takeaways

The Components of Emotional Intelligence (EI): Emotional intelligence comprises five main components – self-awareness, self-regulation, motivation, empathy, and social skills. These traits form the backbone of effective and meaningful interactions, both internally within an organization and externally with customers.

EI translates to increased loyalty and brand advocacy.

Strategies for Infusing EI into Business:

- Training & Development: Implement emotional intelligence training programs across the company.
- Recruitment: Prioritize hiring candidates with evident EI traits.
- Employee Wellbeing: Creating an environment that values emotional health directly contributes to better customer experiences.
- Data-Driven Insights: Use data analytics to gain insights into customer emotions and preferences.

Incorporating these golden nuggets into business strategies can enable organizations to create emotionally resonant interactions, foster deeper connections with their customers, and drive sustainable business growth.

Thank you, Chris Salem for your valuable input!

"Nurturing Dynamic Teams and Empowered Individuals Our People"

Naeim El Zein

Naeim El Zein serves as the Founder and CEO of Mira-Clé, a preeminent training and consulting company operating in Lebanon since 2009 and the UAE since 2022. He also held the position of Partner & COO at iLead Group, a distinguished firm specializing in Leadership & Communication Development. Prior to this, Naeim held pivotal roles, notably as the GS Manager at Kuwait Energy Company (Oil & Gas) with multiple critical HR functions under the GS umbrella, and as the Admin & HR Manager at Al Houkair & Sons Group. With a rich background spanning over two decades, he possesses exceptional expertise in HR Development, Organizational Cultures, Behavioral Psychology, Strategy, and Inter/Intrapersonal Skill Advancement. In his current capacity, Naeim is a distinguished and seasoned trainer and coach for executives and prominent public figures. His transformative training has benefited over 10,000 professionals, and he provides consulting services focused on Human Resources, Strategy, and Workplace Safety to more than 500 clients across the Middle East. His expertise spans business acumen and soft skills, encompassing Influential Communication, Training of Trainers, Public Speaking Excellence, Leadership Mastery, Emotional Intelligence Enhancement, Customer Service Psychology, Behavioral Psychology relating to Body Language, and Microexpressions.

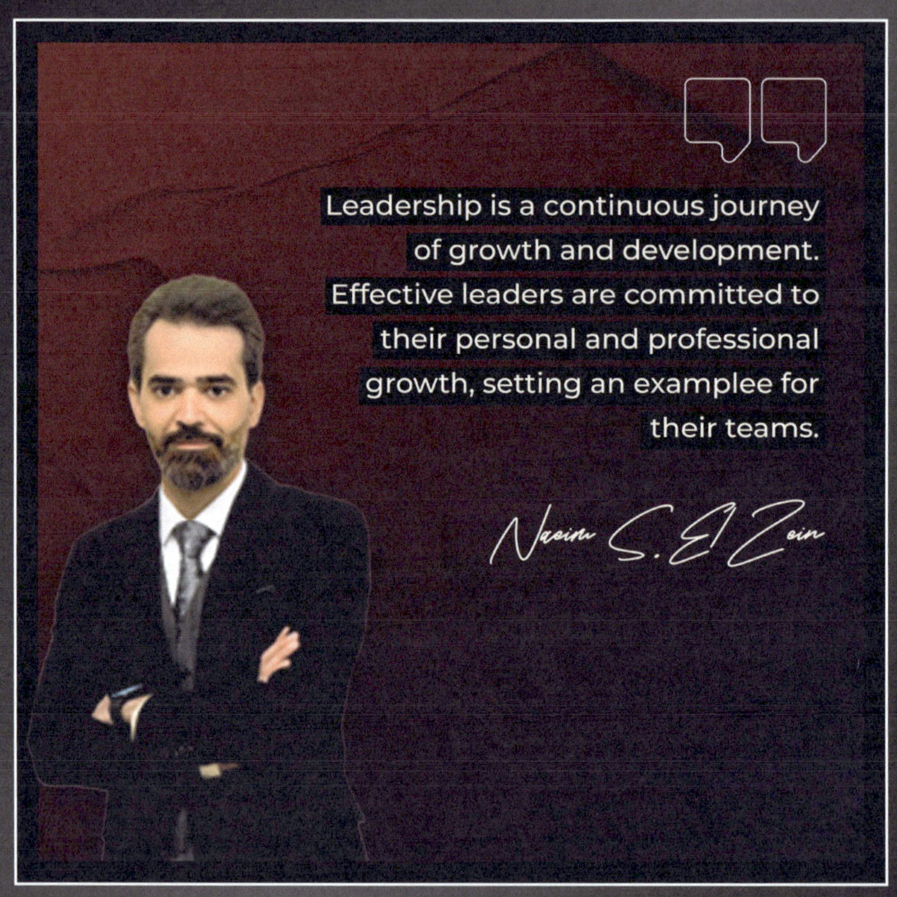

"Treat your men as you would your own beloved sons.
And they will follow you into the deepest valley."

SUN TZU

Turning my modest Human Resources insights into practical takeaways, this chapter provides applied tactics inspired by the transformative journey of nurturing individuals and teams.

It uncovers tried-and-true strategies that empower business leaders to orchestrate excellence within their organizations. Embracing the Human Connection - Bridging Communication Gaps amidst the discord of our fast-paced lives, where stress emanates from rapid changes, the enduring impact of the pandemic, the rule of poor leadership, and the ripples of economic fluctuations, the true meaning of human communication can be overshadowed.

I have personally witnessed these challenges firsthand, consulting and supporting organizations across diverse sectors. In these experiences, I've observed how the relentless hustle often leaves teams overwhelmed and disconnected, their relationships strained both internally and externally, both professionally and personally.

A key challenge lies in preserving empathy and understanding, cornerstones of effective collaboration between teams and their members.

However, the solution emerges from a widely recognized perspective, albeit underrated by several organizations: nurturing emotional intelligence (EI).

Numerous supporting research studies have indicated that up to 90% of top performers share a common characteristic – high EI – surpassing even IQ.

Drawing from my direct involvement, I've had the privilege of witnessing the transformative power of this journey.

By guiding teams back to the essence of their humanity, we've embarked on a shared exploration of experiences, emotions, and vulnerabilities.

Through these tailored processes, leaders and teams have not only learned to communicate authentically but have also undergone a profound shift in perspective.

This shift has empowered them to collectively navigate challenges, foster innovation, adapt to change, embrace diversity, and cultivate a culture of open dialogue.

Just envision a professional setting marked by a culture of open hearts and open minds, all nurtured by the very methods I observed in action.

In my extensive experience, I've found that it is not merely about imparting skills; it is about igniting a transformation that extends far beyond professional boundaries.

Never have organizations been more compelled to integrate emotional intelligence tools, practices, and principles into every facet of their HR strategies. I've seen how this integration spans across each HR function and resonates at the very heart of a company's values and at the heart of its leadership.

The results observed include tangible shifts towards positive communication cultures, increased performance, and effective collaboration – a testament to the importance of nurturing emotional intelligence within today's organizations.

The Learning Odyssey - Adapting in the Face of Rapid Change As technological advancements march forward at an unprecedented pace, skills become obsolete within the blink of an eye.

Acknowledging this, business leaders must tackle the challenge of continuous learning.

The realization that skill sets can decay within three to five years, magnified by the relentless pace of technological progress, demands a fresh approach.

To thrive in this dynamic landscape, a learning culture that thrives on urgency and adaptability must be cultivated.

Swift access to updated learning solutions is pivotal, but the true innovation lies in fostering partnerships with forward-thinking training providers.

These collaborations introduce teams to a diverse pool of trainers, trainers from across the globe, those who became on similar lanes, enabling them to access real-time, evolving content. Such an agile approach empowers teams to become lifelong learners, equipping them with the tools to remain at the forefront of change.

Unveiling the Burnout Paradox - Redefining Resilience. However, amidst the pursuit of growth and adaptability, a formidable challenge emerges: team burnout.

As the demands of modern life intensify, burnout has become an epidemic, casting a shadow over team dynamics and overall productivity. The solution lies not in pushing harder but in redefining resilience. Innovative strategies are required to address burnout's root causes. Empowering teams with techniques for stress management, work-life integration, and mindfulness is crucial.

The journey involves reshaping the organizational culture to prioritize well-being, offering flexible work arrangements, and fostering an environment where self-care is not just encouraged but celebrated. This transformative approach to resilience instills the vitality needed to navigate challenges without sacrificing well-being.

Daring Unconventional Solutions: A retreat to rejuvenation amid the conversation around burnout, an intriguing question surfaces: Have organizations dared to venture into innovative solutions to lead to burnout? Imagine bespoke two-week retreat programs designed for leaders on the brink of burnout. With meticulous pre-program consultations by a team of psychologists, dietitians, life coaches, and well-being therapists, these retreats offer a profound rejuvenation of both energy and mind.

Such well-being retreats stand as a beacon of hope for leaders struggling with burnout and even depression. Consider the ripple effects of burnout on productivity, the toll it takes on peers and subordinates, and the potential loss of vision and direction.

The cost of ignoring burnout's consequences is monumental. Yet, the solution might lie in a reasonable investment in tailored programs that provide a respite for leaders, reigniting their passion and drive.

By redefining resilience in this innovative manner, organizations can safeguard their most valuable asset: their people. Leadership practices in the realm of nurturing individuals and teams, the role of effective leadership practices cannot be overstated. Leaders serve as the guiding force, steering organizations through the ever-changing currents of today's business world.

They hold the torch that illuminates the path to a brighter and more prosperous future - they don't hold a title, titled leader!

As I've crossed diverse industries and cultures over the years, I've witnessed firsthand the pivotal role of true leadership practices in shaping the destiny of organizations.

I'll share modest insights and strategies gleaned from years of observing leaders who harnessed the power of their roles to elevate their teams and, consequently, their organizations and leaders who have inspired me as we worked the path together.

True Leaders, first and foremost, provide an inspirational vision that unites their teams with a compelling purpose and direction.

They create a shared aspiration that fuels motivation and commitment, essential in a world where change is a constant companion.

They share their leadership, and they don't just hold on to it! Effective leaders understand that communication goes beyond conveying information; they know it is about fostering genuine human-empowering connections.

They prioritize open, honest, and authentic communication, creating an environment where team members know they are heard and valued, not just stipulate it, especially in a digital world where meaningful interactions can be elusive. In the face of relentless change, authentic leaders display adaptive agility.

They promote a culture of experimentation and emphasize learning from failures, showcasing resilience in the face of adversity.

Adaptability has consistently remained a non-negotiable leadership trait. The world has witnessed massive companies falling apart; a common thread among them was their reluctance to adapt to or embrace the lessons from failure. It is a part of human nature to encounter failures at certain points, but genuine leadership lies in transforming team members' failures into valuable lessons learned and future success factors.

True leaders know that diversity is not just a buzzword; they know it is a wellspring of strength for organizations.

Inclusive leaders recognize the value of diverse perspectives and actively seek them out. They create an environment where every team member, regardless of background or identity, feels included and empowered to contribute.

They know that the only disability or inability lies in the boundaries they practice when they question the value of diversity.

Great leaders empower others by recognizing their potential and providing them with the autonomy and support to excel – in simple words, they are not pinned to their chairs.

Empowerment unleashes creativity and initiative, resulting in higher levels of engagement and performance.

Leaders who prioritize empowerment create a culture of ownership and accountability, and create other leaders – that's perhaps one true definition of leadership. Leadership is a continuous journey of growth and development.

Effective leaders are committed to their personal and professional growth, setting an example for their teams. They seek opportunities for learning, whether through formal education, mentorship, or self-reflection.

By embodying a growth mindset, leaders inspire a culture of learning and improvement throughout the organization. I've learned that it can be extraordinarily complex to explain the practices of good leadership to someone who has previously held a leadership title, but it becomes relatively straightforward when shared with someone who appreciates the opportunity, the role, and has a genuine intent to convey it to others.

Furthermore, I've also learned that even extraordinarily complex endeavors can become more straightforward with the appropriate level of coaching and support.

Cultivating Empowered Futures: A Legacy of Excellence The journey of nurturing individuals and teams will always be a continuous endeavor, one that requires dedication, adaptability, and innovative thinking.

As the challenges evolve, so must the solutions. The power lies in embracing the core of humanity while equipping teams with skills that transcend technological advancements. In a world marked by both justifiable and unjustifiable complexities, cultivating emotional intelligence, nurturing a culture of humanity within organizations, and fostering an ethos of continuous learning are the pillars of success.

As we chart the course ahead, we will consistently have the opportunity to cultivate an environment where collaboration, empathy, and adaptability converge to shape empowered individuals who thrive amidst change and challenge.

This transformative journey is not solely about cultivating teams; it is about nurturing a legacy of excellence that will endure the test of time!

Coach MJ's Firepower Takeaways

The importance of nurturing emotional intelligence within organizations cannot be overstated. High levels of EI lead to more authentic communication, a shift in perspective, better adaptability, and a culture of open dialogue. These factors are paramount in ensuring teams can navigate challenges and drive innovation.

Continuous Learning in a Rapidly Changing Landscape: With technological advancements rendering skills obsolete at an unprecedented pace, businesses must foster a culture of continuous learning.

Forming partnerships with forward-thinking training providers introduces teams to a globally diverse pool of trainers, ensuring they remain at the forefront of change.

Addressing the Burnout Paradox & Redefining Resilience: As burnout becomes more prevalent, the solution lies in not pushing teams harder but in redefining resilience and self-care.

Innovative solutions, such as retreat programs for rejuvenating leaders, can be an effective way to tackle burnout head-on.

Authentic Leadership Practices: True leadership is about providing an inspirational vision, fostering genuine human connections, and showcasing adaptability.

Cultivating a Legacy of Excellence: The journey to nurturing dynamic teams is ongoing and demands dedication, adaptability, and innovative thinking.

By integrating these golden nuggets into office practices, organizations can foster more cohesive, empowered, and resilient teams, ultimately driving greater productivity and success.

Well done, Naeim El Zein!

"Unleashing Your Unstoppable Potential: Breaking Through the Psychological Barriers to Success"

Dr. Robyn Odegaard

Dr. Robyn is a former competitive beach volleyball player turned high performance psychologist with continuing education in nutrition.

She has written three books and given a TEDx talk titled *Creating Success out of Chaos*. Her clients call her a "smoke jumper" because she "parachutes in and helps fight life's fires from the inside."

She has facilitated more than 330 episodes of her panel discussion video podcast called '*Quick Hits*' because she adores the intellectual stimulation of a good conversation.

In her spare time, she reads astrophysics for fun, works out, tends to her garden and WAY too many houseplants and trains her dog Nebula to do circus tricks.

As a highly sought-after Executive Coach serving celebrities, CEOs, and sports stars, she is often referred to as the 'MacGyver' because of his acute ability to understand and process real-life complexities.

"To attain knowledge, add things every day. To attain wisdom, subtract things every day."

LAO TZU

Head trash, the voice in your head, psychological barriers, chaos.

No matter what you call it, everyone striving to reach and maintain peak performance deals with it.

Unfortunately for most of us, we try to manage it alone.

We might feel shame or frustration that our own head is the thing that gets in our way. In this chapter, you will discover a trailblazing approach to overcoming the mental, emotional, and psychological obstacles that keep you from achieving and maintaining your highest potential.

Welcome to a transformative realm where chaos is tamed, hurdles become stepping stones, and your success awaits.

Peak performance is not a destination; it is a way of life. The Head Trash of Fear: You must break through fear to achieve success – or not. There are two kinds of fear. We hear a lot about the first one. The fear that holds us back keeps us from being bold and keeps us playing small.

I call this trauma-based fear. Somewhere in your past, someone told you to play it safe. "Be careful! You might get hurt." "Don't try that. You'll look foolish if you fail."

Maybe you did try, and it didn't work out as planned.

Maybe someone who was supposed to love you and to look out for your best interest said, "I told you so." This can lead to feelings of shame and regret.

The human brain is really good at internalizing and learning from those experiences. It wants to keep you safe.

That kind of fear absolutely needs to be overcome, broken through and passed if you want to play big and achieve at the highest level. And there is another kind of fear.

This fear is your intuition or "gut feeling" trying to keep you from doing something stupid. It is the part of your brain that doesn't have access to language (more on that in a bit) desperately trying to get a message across telling you to STOP!

That isn't a good idea. That's the kind of fear we should listen to and heed. Confuse them or mix them up to your own peril. Early in my business I confused them and walked through fear I should have listened to. That mistake cost me $20k and months of wasted time working with a vendor who turned out to be a complete shyster. How do you tell the difference?

There isn't an easy one-size-fits-all answer. Knowing these different fears exist and feel very similar is a start.

Ask yourself what the voice in your head is saying. Often all we have is the feeling. There aren't actual words.

That is because the emotional side of your brain doesn't have access to language. Unfortunately, the logical side of your brain only has access to language, and when it gets "fear" messages it wants to know, "Fight? Flight? Freeze?"

The only way to sort out what kind of fear you're having is to talk out loud about it (for some people journaling also works).

Talk to yourself in a mirror. Talk to a video camera. Open a Zoom meeting and talk to yourself. Even better, have conversation with a credible confidant--someone you trust to be able to keep up with you (you are super smart and tend to lose people when you try to process with them).

Look for someone who will ask you good questions and can notice the nuances between these two types of fear.

Watch out for people who will strongly take one side or the other.

If they are all about "listen to your intuition!" or "bust through the fear!" They are not good sounding boards.

Summary – There are two types of fear: trauma-based fear you must break through and intuition-based fear you must listen to.

Telling the difference is critical to high performance.

The Head Trash of Overwhelm: No one can do it as well as you can – or can they?

Do any or all these words feel as if they could describe your daily grind? Overworked? Overwhelmed?

Underutilized. Undervalued. Underestimated. You aren't alone.

Every high performer I have worked with, it doesn't matter if he/she is a founder, executive, celebrity, or pro-athlete, has connected with the image of stagnation and frustration those words invoke.

Let's look at each issue in turn: Overworked and Overwhelmed – too much to do and not enough time. If you ever feel the need to say, "I don't have time." Change it to, "That isn't a priority." How does that feel? Is it a gut-punch?

If yes, that thing is a priority. If your response is more like, "Eh, I guess it is not." You can decide if you are going to delegate it or just let it slide.

I have a rule that if something gets moved from one list to another three times and I don't do it, I have to decide there and then if I am going to do it, delegate it, or let it go.

When I decide to let things go, I don't allow the head-trash of guilt to creep in. That one rule has made a dramatic difference in my feeling overworked and overwhelmed.

Underutilized: You are spending too much time doing menial things and not enough time in your zone of genius.

What are you really good at? What are the things only you can do? And don't tell me "Everything." I don't believe you.

(See the Foresting Project below to help you discover your zone of genius.) If you think you are the only person who can do a task that is not related to your unique creativity and zone of genius, it means you haven't created a good standard operating procedure (SOP).

I have confronted many CEOs on this issue even going so far as to sit next to them and take notes with the bet on the table that if I could do the thing to 80% accuracy at the end, it meant it wasn't in their zone of genius and they needed to delegate it.

Make a point to spend as much of your time as possible in your zone of genius. And let go of mindless, busy work tasks you can train someone else to do. This includes business and personal stuff. These are some things you might not think about contributing to feeling underutilized: Travel arrangements (do YOU need to go to that conference?) including vacation planning, laundry, managing yard/pool/housekeeping staff, business and personal bookkeeping, sales/marketing, hiring/training/firing employees, and board of director management, etc.

Of course, all of that assumes you actually know what your zone of genius is. If you don't, that's the place to start. What are the things you REALLY enjoy doing?

The things that put you into flow. That you could do all day every day and be thrilled about it. That is your zone of genius. Find ways to live in that space every day.

Undervalued and Underestimated: This is an issue with your social network.

The people who are closest to you don't understand you. They think you work too hard for too little reward.

They can't see the big picture. When you try to explain it to them, they have a million reasons why you will fail---you'll get sued or the idea is pointless.

Sadly, this often comes from a significant other or people you consider friends. You might hear that you aren't doing enough around the house even though you feel like you are contributing. You might be told that what you are doing isn't done "right."

Something big and exciting happens at work and you really want to celebrate, but when you share it, you get a barrage of fear based on "did you think about this?" and "what about that?" questions.

People who love you, or are at least supposed to love you, are trying to keep you safe from THEIR fears. It is exhausting to feel as if you have to manage their emotions while also keeping yourself pumped up and driving forward.

Summary: Feelings of being overworked, overwhelmed, underutilized, undervalued, and underestimated are normal and common among high achievers.

You get to decide if you are going to let those feelings continue or do something to change them. The Head Trash of Self-Sabotage: Ignoring Your Health In his book, The Big Leap, Gay Hendricks talks about how each of us is given an upper limit in childhood.

Early in life, someone convinces our unconscious mind that we are only allowed to be so successful or make a certain amount of money.

When we get close to that limit, we do things that sabotage our progress and bring us back to the perceived safety of our limiting beliefs.

The most common form of self-sabotage I see in high performers is driving their physical body ridiculously hard while simultaneously treating it horribly. They don't exercise, get enough sleep, or fuel their bodies well.

They drink too much, may use drugs (prescription or otherwise), engage in risky sexual practices, and are adrenaline junkies doing dangerous things for the bravado and the rush.

This is the perfect recipe for allowing yourself to get sick or injured, which is a great excuse for being stuck in the mediocre middle or even failing.

It is your responsibility as someone who wants to be successful in managing your health and safety. It is absolutely self-sabotage to behave as if your physical body and mental well-being can be ignored and beaten to the ground without consequence.

I will give one example without belaboring the point: Steve Jobs. Do better. Don't hold yourself back by driving yourself to the point where your body shuts down and forces you to take an unscheduled break. Or worse, you end up in an early grave.

Summary: Your health is your number one asset, and you get to control how you treat your body and your mental health.

Not taking care of yourself is self-sabotage, and you will never reach your big goals.

Overcoming Head Trash: The solution, The cause of your current situation is in the past.

Some of it is the distant past: your family of origin, your education, your life experience. There are times when it makes sense to look at the history we carry with us---things like the default ways we communicate or engage in conflict and what we unconsciously believe about ourselves and what we deserve in the world.

It may not be your fault, but it is your problem.

By examining the origins of our negative self-talk, we can make conscious and purposeful choices about if those automatic responses and behaviors are serving our adult selves.

The solution is in the present. The easiest thing to do is to allow today to become a continuation of yesterday.

Which means there is no hope of your future being different from your past. For tomorrow to be different, we have to make a change today.

The motivation is in the future. Your future self is someone you do not yet know. As humans we are less likely to do hard things for people we don't know.

To find the motivation to make changes today, ask yourself, "What do I want to be different?" Take your answer to that question and use it to develop a plan that will energize you to create and maintain the changes you want to see.

You don't have to do it on your own, but you do have to do it. Your future self will thank you.

Summary: The cause is in the past.

The solution is in the present. The motivation is in the future.

The Foresting Project: An overarching way to sort what you think and feel about everything and create change. This exercise will allow you to break down your life into distinct areas that you can then look at one at a time.

By visualizing these areas as separate trees in the forest that is your life, you will be able to assess and prioritize them individually, enabling you to identify which trees need fertilizer or water (more focus), pruning (change or less focus), or even removal (self-explanatory).

This is best done with a coach or confidant who can ask good questions and keep you accountable for the answers.

But you can get reasonable insights by doing it on your own if you must.

I like to do this with index cards, yes real pieces of paper.

I have even done it with clients virtually and then mailed them the cards at the end.

If your handwriting is awful or you'd just rather use software, go for it.

You can't really do this wrong. What you'll need: Index cards of assorted colors – size depends on how big your handwriting is and how verbose you are A writing utensil of choice – a favor pen is wonderful.

Multiple colors if that's your thing A feeling words list (there are many online for free) Be warned: You are going to end up with A LOT of cards!

That's the point.

Your life has a lot going on and you are the cog holding the Venn Diagram of moving parts together.

That is exactly what we are trying to look at and get a handle on.

Be patient with yourself while also committing to do the work.

It won't help you if you don't do it.

How it works: Let us start with your work life.

Choose a color card and write "Work People" on it.

Now create one card in that color for each person you interact with regularly. This could be board members, employees, peers, vendors, your coach, etc.

Choose a different color card and write "Work Tasks" on it.

Make a card in that color for all the things you do. If you have trouble here, look at your calendar and see how you spend your time.

Do not forget thinking and creative time and the "silly little things" you do like take out trash. Now look at each card.

On the back write how much time you spend each week on the person or task. Would you like to spend more or less time on it?

What comes up for you when you think about this person or task? How do you feel? What does the voice in your head have to say about it?

This could be in sentence form or just words. The feeling words list will be hugely helpful in getting your emotional brain and logical brain to communicate.

If you think of work categories beyond people and tasks, include them. Now your personal life. You might need more colors here because there are likely more categories e.g.: volunteering, childcare, social life, church/ spiritual life, support people – therapist, housekeeper, lawn person, family – immediate and extended, significant other, pets, personal health – exercise/diet/meditation, sleep (you must have one for sleep), etc.

Be creative about how you categorize things. If a category has people or tasks associated with it, make a card in that color for each person/task.

For example, under your immediate family, you might make one for your significant other and each of your children or maybe your parents and each sibling.

Or it might be all the above. Once you feel as if you've got most of the people and tasks in your life listed, do the same exercise on the back as you did for work.

When you think about the task/person on the card, how much time each week are you spending on it? Do you want to spend more or less time on it?

What comes up for you? How do you feel? What does the voice in your head have to say? Don't silence it. Listen and write it down.

Again, use the feelings word list. What did this exercise bring up for you? If you are like a lot of my clients, you are realizing that you have WAY more time written on the back of the cards than there actually is in a week.

Where do you want to spend more time? Which things are time-sinks that you could change? Which cards have happy, joyful words on the back, and which are less positive? Who are your go-to people and who are draining you?

This process will also help you discover your zone of genius. The things you are good at and love to do will become clear based on what you write on the back of the cards. Knowing what you know now, what needs to change?

Summary: Doing the Foresting Project will give you a clear understanding of where you are spending your time and how you feel about it. The process might feel daunting at first. Take your time. It doesn't all have to be done in one sitting. Commit to doing it.

Your future self will thank you.

Head Trash: Final Thoughts: In this chapter, I have invited you to embark on a profound journey of self-discovery, personal growth, and professional expansion.

As you navigate the intricate landscape of your own mind, I stand beside you as your steadfast ally.

By understanding and confronting the fears that hold you back, by reclaiming your time and embracing your unique strengths, and by prioritizing your well-being, you pave the way for a life of unparalleled achievement, fulfillment, and happiness.

The path is not always easy, but it is undeniably worth the adventure.

Remember, the cause is in the past, the solution is in the present, and the motivation is in the future.

So go forth with confidence, armed with the tools and insights that this journey provided. Your future self awaits your triumphant arrival.

Coach MJ's Firepower Takeaways

Navigating the Two Fears: Understand the distinction between trauma-based fear, born from past events holding you back, and intuition-based fear, serving as an internal alarm. To truly discern between them, engage in open discussions with trusted allies. Making accurate judgments between these fears is the cornerstone of peak performance.

Mastering the Overwhelm: Whenever you're tempted to say, "I don't have time," pivot to "That isn't a priority." This simple shift can spotlight your genuine priorities. Introduce effective management tactics like deciding on the fate of repeatedly postponed tasks to drastically diminish feelings of overwhelm.

Unlocking Your Zone of Genius: Strive to allocate the majority of your time to tasks that play to your unique strengths or your "zone of genius." If you're clinging to a task believing only you can execute it, it's time to reevaluate and establish robust standard operating procedures. Delegating tasks outside of your genius zone can lead to optimal utilization of your talents and diminish feelings of being sidelined.

Championing Health & Well-being: A frequent pitfall for high achievers is neglecting their physical and mental health, which doesn't just hamper performance but can also cut your journey short. Commit to routine health check-ins and nurture both body and mind, recognizing that your health is your most prized asset on your success journey.

Harnessing the Foresting Project for Crystal Clear Focus: Systematically break down your life's sectors, like work assignments or personal tasks, using a visual tool like index cards. This deep dive can illuminate how your time is being spent and your emotional response to each duty. The insights from this exercise can guide you to a more productive and fulfilling allocation of your time and energy.

By embracing these favorite takeaways, individuals can tackle internal barriers that frequently stand in the way of success, ensuring they consistently perform at their zenith.

Thank you, Dr. Robyn!

"Data's Transformative Firepower: Igniting Action and Achieving Results"

Dr. Joe Perez

Dr. Joe Perez, an award-winning thought leader, prolific international keynote speaker, and published author with 40+ years in IT and education has amassed an impressive portfolio. From Business Intelligence Specialist to Senior Systems Analyst and fractional CTO, he's an authority in data viz/analytics and process improvement. Featured on a Times Square billboard, he's a powerhouse of expertise, integrity, and excellence. As a recognized Thought Leader in business networks such as LinkedIn, Perez sparks innovation, captivating audiences at conferences in 20-plus countries worldwide.

"As the mariner relies on the stars to traverse the vast sea, so too must man rely on acquired knowledge to navigate the course of his endeavors."

ARISTOTLE

In November of 2017, Carnival Cruises embarked on a journey that exemplified the true firepower of data. They introduced the Ocean Medallion, a revolutionary wearable device that would forever alter the way passengers experienced their voyages. This innovation wasn't just about convenience; it was a strategic fusion of data and technology that ignited a transformation in customer service. The Ocean Medallion effortlessly unlocked cabin doors, orchestrated culinary delights, recommended personalized activities, and tailored entertainment options based on individual preferences and location. Beyond these conveniences, it enabled the crew to monitor passenger satisfaction in real-time, responding swiftly to requests and concerns. This daring embrace of big data wasn't just an investment; it was a profound recognition of data's potency.

In the dynamic landscape of modern business, this story encapsulates the formidable force that data represents. Much like a well-armed battalion's firepower, data holds the potential to equip organizations with the tools needed to achieve their goals. As we dive into the depths of data's boundless potential in this chapter, we find ourselves at a crossroads, ready to harness its might and guide the future of business. Just as Carnival Cruises leveraged data to craft personalized experiences that enhanced loyalty and revenue, we, too, are poised to explore the ways data can shape strategies, refine decision-making, and illuminate paths to triumph for businesses and individuals alike.

Equipping Organizations with Data Firepower for Success

Data, once confined to spreadsheets and databases, has transcended its origins to become a dynamic force in driving results. The parallels between data's evolution and an organization's capability for action (its firepower, if you will) are striking; both demand skill, precision, and an astute awareness of their potential. The art lies in taking raw data, much like a skilled marksman carefully selects and loads ammunition for their target pistol, and then deftly leveraging it into a potent tool for achieving desired outcomes.

Drawing from my decades of experience in analytics, business intelligence, systems analysis, and data management, I've witnessed the transformation of data from mere digits to a strategic asset. Just as an organization marshals its firepower for decisive action, data is reshaping business landscapes in remarkable ways. The task isn't merely to collect data but to orchestrate it into a strategic symphony that drives decisions and propels innovation.

As Peter Sondergaard, Senior Vice President and Global Head of Research at Gartner, Inc., aptly put it, "Information is the oil of the 21st century, and analytics is the combustion engine." This sentiment aligns seamlessly with the concept of data as the modern-day firepower, where information is the ammunition and analytics serves as the precision-engineered mechanism that propels organizations forward. Just as a well-tuned engine drives a vehicle with precision, skillful data analytics empower organizations to navigate the ever-evolving landscapes of business with confidence and purpose, wielding their data firepower to overcome challenges and seize opportunities.

Charting the Future: Innovation, AI, and Emerging Technologies

As we peer into the future, it blazes with the promise of innovation, fueled by technologies that harness data's full potential. Artificial Intelligence (AI) emerges as a torchbearer, deciphering intricate patterns within vast datasets that human cognition would grapple to unravel on its own. Analogous to an organization's firepower in times of need, AI elevates our capacity to extract value from the vast sea of big data, enabling predictive analytics, personalization, and automation on an unparalleled scale.

However, the journey transcends AI; it hinges on a comprehensive data approach. Data streams from various sources, such as internal databases, third-party providers, and real-time IoT sensors, converge to create a foundation for all-encompassing insights. This forges a tapestry of knowledge that guides business strategies.

Moreover, data's potency extends into the realm of ethics. Similar to an organization's moral compass guiding its actions, ethical considerations in data usage loom large. In an era where data privacy, security, and transparency reign, organizations must wield data's might conscientiously, ensuring that the potential for results doesn't inadvertently compromise integrity. Cat Coode, the Founder of Binary Tattoo, once said, "Technology is not the problem; it is how we use it that matters." These words echo the sentiment expressed in this section, reminding us that technology's impact rests not in its existence but in how we harness its capabilities for the greater good.

Guiding the Journey to the Future

So, how do we navigate this ever-evolving landscape of data's potential? Much like a seasoned navigator steering a vessel, I approach this challenge holistically, informed by my career path as an educator, IT expert, and data storyteller. I passionately believe in the art of data storytelling, akin to a master strategist formulating battle plans. Just as the strategist envisions scenarios and anticipates outcomes, I strive to craft data narratives that equip decision-makers with actionable insights. In my experience, I've seen the potency of data-driven stories that resonate across diverse audiences. I will elaborate on this concept later.

This chapter explores how data's potential, likened to an organization's firepower, can drive transformative business endeavors. From igniting innovation through AI to ensuring ethical governance, my intent is to illuminate the path for businesses eager to wield data's potency conscientiously.

In a world where data's radiance unveils uncharted territories, my goal is for this chapter to serve as a strategic guide, leading readers to a future where data isn't merely a tool but a catalyst for action and achievement. Just as an organization's firepower influences its destiny, data's influence on the future of business is poised to be transformative.

In reflecting upon this, a vivid tale emerges – a story of opportunity and consequence. In the year 1984, the NBA draft unfolded in a way that demonstrated the perils of ignoring data-driven insights. The Portland Trail Blazers held the second overall pick and selected Sam Bowie, a promising center from the University of Kentucky. Aligned with the prevailing trends, they opted for an elite big man, expecting to strengthen their team roster. Bowie's college statistics were respectable, yet injuries ultimately marred his NBA journey, leading to a trade years later.

However, as history would reveal, the Chicago Bulls seized the third overall pick and made a different choice. In a testament to the power of informed decision-making, they selected Michael Jordan based upon insights they were able to derive from the information available about his performance and track record in the sport up to that point. The trajectory of the franchise was forever altered by that one decision. Jordan went on to become one of the greatest basketball players of all time, clinching six NBA championships and five MVP awards.

This narrative illustrates how the absence of data-driven analysis can lead to misguided choices. The Blazers' decision, while seeming to be logical at the time, overlooked the potential insights data could offer. The ramifications were profound as they missed the opportunity to secure a future legend, Michael Jordan, due to the absence of data-informed decision-making.

The lesson from this tale echoes in the realm of data-driven business decisions. Just as the Blazers' choice had a lasting impact, our decisions today have the potential to shape the future of our organizations. Embracing data as a guiding light is paramount, ensuring that we harness its transformative potential to chart courses that lead to prosperity and success.

Together, we'll traverse this unknown landscape, leveraging data's potential and guiding businesses into the dawn of a new era, where the lessons of history intertwine with the promise of data-driven futures.

Translating Data into Insights That Drive Action

As we navigate the terrain of data-driven decisions, the process of transforming data into actionable insights becomes our guiding beacon through the haze of information overload. Think of this process as though it were an adventure, an overseas expedition. Much like an explorer who relies on maps and compasses in uncharted territory, I rely on a structured process to convert raw data into the compass that steers strategic endeavors.

The journey starts by defining the problem: an expedition into the business landscape to pinpoint the challenges that necessitate data-driven insights. In this role, picture yourself acting as a contemporary cartographer, mapping out the contours of the issue at hand. By dissecting the challenge into manageable components, you set the stage for an exhaustive data collection strategy.

The second phase mirrors the explorer's task of gathering tools and supplies. In this context, data becomes the toolkit: an arsenal of information holding the keys to deciphering complexities. We must plunge into data streams, extracting knowledge from internal databases, third-party providers, and real-time sources. This step echoes my belief in casting a wide net, leaving no valuable nugget of information undiscovered.

Similar to an alchemist refining base metals into gold, the next phase involves cleansing and preparing the data. Much like an experienced traveler assembling provisions, it is necessary to scrub raw data to ensure accuracy, comprehensiveness, and uniformity. By filtering out noise and rectifying inconsistencies, we lay the groundwork for reliable data, which is an essential resource for unearthing meaningful insights.

With a well-equipped toolkit in hand, the expedition now takes an analytical turn. This phase mirrors the explorer's careful observation of the terrain. As we dive into the data, our goal is to identify patterns, correlations, and anomalies. Data visualization becomes my compass, helping to navigate the intricate landscape of data relationships. These visualizations, reminiscent of landmarks on an explorer's map, guide decision-makers toward valuable insights.

Just as an explorer relies on tried-and-true navigation instruments, this is where statistical models and machine learning algorithms should be deployed. The voyage transforms into a quest for hidden treasures; that is, insights lying beneath the surface, awaiting discovery. Similar to an explorer deciphering enigmatic maps, we must translate data's language into actionable recommendations, shedding light on previously unseen pathways.

And here's where the threads of our narrative intertwine with a remarkable tale of research. According to a groundbreaking 2016 study led by MIT professors and involving nearly 200 manufacturing plants across North America and Europe, the connection between data-driven decision-making and increased productivity became clear. These findings, akin to the treasures uncovered by explorers, revealed a statistically significant increase of 3% or more in productivity, on average, with greater use of data-driven strategies. What's more intriguing is that these improvements were observed only after plants actively adopted data-driven decision-making (DDD), echoing the journey we've embarked upon, where the application of data transforms into real-world impact.

Continuing with the "explorer" metaphor, and in tandem with an explorer's unwavering reliance on navigation instruments, these revelations validate the significance of our analytical approach. Similar to the explorers' deciphering of data to unveil hidden routes, we translate data's intricate language into actionable insights, navigating the complexities of business with precision.

As our voyage reaches its pinnacle, validation serves as the ultimate test, much like an explorer assessing the waters for reliability. In data's realm, validation confirms the effectiveness of models and insights. Stringent testing and validation protocols serve as gatekeepers, allowing only the most accurate and reliable insights to guide decision-makers, much like explorers who trust only in the most reliable tools for their journeys.

The saga we've explored together speaks to the transformative potential of data-driven decisions. Just as explorers once ventured into the unknown, armed with maps and instruments, we, too, ventured into the uncharted territories of business, equipped with data as our guiding star. In this grand adventure, data's transformation into insights becomes our compass, steering us toward the future where actionable knowledge shapes our destiny.

Nurturing a Robust Data Warehouse for Capability

Having translated data into actionable insights and considering the importance of properly storing it, like a well-stocked armory powering a battalion, a data warehouse fuels an organization's operations by efficiently storing, managing, and delivering data. A smoothly running data warehouse is like a powerful engine. Just as an engine seamlessly propels a vehicle forward, a flexible data warehousing architecture efficiently manages, stores, and delivers data to drive informed decision-making.

In the same manner that an engine's various components must work together seamlessly to ensure optimal performance, so also does a data warehousing architecture require interlocking parts such as data integration, data storage, and data retrieval to perform at its best. Like an engine that can be fine-tuned for specific driving conditions, a flexible data warehousing architecture can be adjusted to accommodate changes in an organization's data needs, allowing for smooth operation even in the face of shifting demands.

Navigating these challenges while maintaining a balanced approach is crucial. Just as an organization must safeguard sensitive information while ensuring authorized access, meticulous data governance policies and robust security measures play a pivotal role. This realm of expertise that I have developed over decades of experience in business intelligence and data warehousing forms the foundation of best practices in this domain that I strongly advocate.

Addressing data accuracy and consistency is paramount, resembling an organization's need for precise execution. Derived decisions are only as reliable as the data from which they stem. The implementation of rigorous data quality controls is akin to a blacksmith meticulously crafting essential tools. The process refines and standardizes data, setting the stage for trustworthy insights.

Moreover, the concept of a unified data repository aligns seamlessly with the blacksmith's workshop: a place where various materials are centralized for efficient use. The data warehouse serves as the heart of data-driven operations, accommodating diverse data types and sources. Navigating this repository necessitates a deep understanding of data architecture, reminiscent of the blacksmith's mastery of diverse metals.

In this context, and continuing with the blacksmith analogy, let's draw inspiration from a compelling real-world story that mirrors our principles.

In 2019, a leading software company, VIP, faced challenges like those encountered in the realm of data warehousing. Much like a blacksmith striving for efficiency in the forge, VIP struggled with manually scheduling and monitoring data transfers, leading to inefficiencies and errors in their data delivery processes. They were navigating a landscape akin to a dark and smoky forge. Limited visibility and control over their data pipelines obscured their path forward.

However, their journey toward optimization took a transformative turn, aligning with our commitment to fostering efficiency through automation. VIP chose to embrace a universal automation platform, akin to the evolution of the blacksmith's tools, to orchestrate and automate their data pipelines across different platforms and applications. This change brought about remarkable results:

- They centralized control of data delivery processes, much like a well-stocked workshop, allowing for easy design, execution, and monitoring of data transfers.
- Automated data extraction, transformation, and loading (ETL) processes, akin to the streamlining of a blacksmith's workflow, using predefined connectors and scripts that handled various data formats and protocols.
- Citizen automators, such as business analysts and developers, became empowered to create and manage their own data pipelines, echoing the spirit of the blacksmith's mastery.
- Substantial operational cost savings, parallel to the blacksmith's efficient resource utilization, as manual efforts, errors, and delays were greatly reduced.

The parallels between this story and our principles are striking. Swift data access, enhanced efficiency, and improved agility were outcomes akin to the well-stocked workshop, the blacksmith's optimized workflow, and the adaptability to changing needs and expectations. This story underlines the paramount importance of optimizing data delivery pipelines in today's dynamic business landscape, resonating with our commitment to fostering efficiency through automation.

The saga of VIP's journey to optimization seamlessly integrates with our exploration of a robust data warehousing architecture, highlighting the power of applying principles to real-world scenarios. As the blacksmith refines tools to perfection, we also refine data delivery mechanisms to enable seamless insights, fostering a culture of innovation and adaptability.

Therefore, just as a powerful engine is the key to a successful road trip, a flexible data warehousing architecture is the key to a successful data-driven journey, where principles come alive through transformative tales of innovation.

Crafting Compelling Data Narratives Through Storytelling

Continuing the journey of data's transformative role, an efficient data warehouse lays the foundation for actionable insights. These insights, now accessible for decision-makers, find their conduit through the art of data storytelling. In the realm of data, storytelling emerges as an art; a way to weave raw information into compelling narratives that captivate and inform. This artistry parallels my passion for music, where notes are strung together to create melodies that resonate with emotions. Just as a composer constructs symphonies, you must seek to craft data narratives that harmonize with the needs of diverse audiences.

The art of data storytelling begins with identifying the audience's pulse. This is a task akin to a composer gauging the emotional tenor of the listeners. By understanding the audience's interests, concerns, and objectives, you will be enabled to tailor narratives that speak directly to their hearts and minds.

Continuing with the musical metaphor, the next step is akin to composing the score: a symphony of data points that unfold logically and evocatively. Data visualization becomes a musical notation, guiding the audience through a visual journey. Bar charts, scatter plots, and heat maps are the musical notes, harmonizing to create a narrative that resonates visually. The harmonious alignment of data points mirrors the harmonies that emerge from musical notes.

In the same vein, pacing is crucial, analogous to a conductor's control over the tempo of a piece. Controlling the narrative's rhythm is crucial, thus ensuring that insights are revealed in a way that maintains engagement and builds anticipation. The ebb and flow of the narrative echoes the crescendos and diminuendos of a musical masterpiece.

Furthermore, just as a musical piece reaches its crescendo, a data narrative culminates in a powerful insight or revelation. This "aha" moment mirrors the climactic point of a musical composition, leaving the audience with a sense of fulfillment and enlightenment. It is this transformative experience that I aim to create with each data story I craft: a resonance that stays with the audience long after the narrative concludes.

To illustrate the importance and impact of data storytelling, let me share with you a historical case study that was presented by Brent Dykes, data storytelling expert and author of the book Effective Data Storytelling: How to Drive Change with Data, Narrative, and Visuals. The case study is about Dr. Ignaz Semmelweis, a Hungarian physician who worked at an obstetrics clinic in Vienna in the mid-19th century, where many women died from childbed fever, a post-delivery infection. Semmelweis noticed that the mortality rate of women whose babies were delivered by physicians and medical students was much higher than those whose babies were delivered by midwives.

He hypothesized that the doctors and students were carrying some kind of material from the corpses they dissected to the delivery rooms, causing the infection. He proposed that washing hands with a chlorine solution before attending to patients would reduce the risk of death.

Semmelweis collected data from the clinic and showed that handwashing reduced the mortality rate from 18.3% to 1.2% in just one year. However, he failed to convince his colleagues and superiors of his theory because he did not present his data in a compelling and persuasive way. He simply showed them tables and charts with numbers without providing any context, narrative, or visualization that would appeal to their emotions and logic.

Dykes argued that if Semmelweis had used data storytelling principles, he could have communicated his insights more effectively and saved thousands of lives. He suggested that Semmelweis should have followed a strategic approach in line with the four fundamental steps essential to the art of data storytelling (analogous to the four steps outlined above):

- Identify the audience's pulse: Semmelweis should have sought to understand the specific interests, concerns, and objectives of his primary audience, predominantly composed of fellow doctors who held a high regard for scientific evidence and safeguarding their professional reputation. In adapting his narrative, he should have tailored it to directly address the skepticism and entrenched resistance to change that he encountered.
- Compose the score: To effectively convey his findings, Semmelweis should have harnessed the power of data visualization to guide his audience on a visual journey. Although the advanced tools of today were not available to him in the mid-1800s, he could have utilized the resources at hand to illustrate the connection between handwashing and mortality rates. While bar charts, scatter plots, and

heat maps might have been out of reach, he could have explored creative methods to visually convey the vital correlation between hand hygiene and infection prevention.

- Control the tempo: Semmelweis's narrative should have been paced strategically to maintain engagement and foster anticipation. Gradually revealing his insights, he could have employed techniques such as contrast and comparison to underscore disparities between patient groups. Repetition and emphasis could have reinforced his focal points, enhancing audience understanding and retention.
- Reach the crescendo: Semmelweis should have culminated his narrative with a powerful insight or revelation that would leave the audience with a sense of fulfillment and enlightenment. By highlighting the potential life-saving impact of handwashing, not just within their own clinic but globally, he could have ignited a sense of purpose and urgency. A clear call to action would have impelled his peers to adopt his practice and propagate his message, leading to a transformative shift in medical practices, potentially saving many more lives.

In reflecting upon Semmelweis's historical context, these steps offer a blueprint for how he could have utilized the principles of data storytelling to effect change and innovation, even within the technological limitations of his time.

Unfortunately, Semmelweis' findings were rejected by the medical community at the time he published them in 1861. He died in 1865 after being committed to an asylum by his colleagues. His theory was only accepted years after his death when Louis Pasteur and Joseph Lister confirmed the germ theory and practiced antiseptic methods.

This research study illustrates how data storytelling can be used to put data insights into context for and inspire action from an audience. It shows how data storytelling is an art that parallels music, where notes are strung together to create melodies that resonate with emotions.

Igniting Innovation: Embracing AI and Emerging Technologies

Continuing the expedition through data's multifaceted realm and the narratives that bring it to life, the landscape of innovation stands as a realm of uncharted possibilities, beckoning businesses to harness emerging technologies that redefine the business landscape. Much like a craftsman embracing novel materials and techniques, organizations must forge a path that integrates Artificial Intelligence (AI) and data-driven insights to sculpt their futures.

AI's role in this narrative mirrors the masterful craftsmanship of a sculptor, an artist who shapes raw material into breathtaking forms. AI possesses the same transformative potential, molding vast datasets into actionable insights that guide decisions. Through machine learning algorithms, AI identifies patterns, predicts outcomes, and refines strategies; a symphony of capabilities that resonate with my expertise in data analytics and innovation.

In the realm of healthcare, AI functions as the virtuoso sculptor, shaping vast amounts of medical data into precise diagnostic insights. As American engineer and professor Dr. W. Edwards Deming eloquently stated, "In God we trust, all others bring data." AI adheres to this principle, bringing unparalleled precision to medical diagnosis. For instance, AI-powered algorithms in radiology meticulously analyze medical images, identifying subtle anomalies that might escape human observation. These insights expedite diagnosis, enabling timely interventions and ultimately improving patient outcomes.

Furthermore, AI algorithms can predict disease progression, recommend personalized treatment plans, and optimize medical resource allocation. Consider the case of a patient with Parkinson's disease. AI-powered algorithms can analyze a combination of medical records, genetic information, and sensor data from wearable devices. By assessing patterns in the patient's movement, tremors, and other relevant data, AI can forecast the progression of the disease with a high degree of accuracy.

In this scenario, AI not only predicts disease progression but also assists in tailoring treatment plans. Based on the patient's individual health profile, including factors such as age, genetics, lifestyle, and response to medication, AI can recommend personalized treatment strategies. This level of precision enhances the effectiveness of interventions, ensuring that patients receive the most suitable care.

Moreover, AI's ability to optimize medical resource allocation is exemplified in the allocation of healthcare professionals and equipment. By analyzing historical patient admission patterns and predicting future demand, AI can help hospitals allocate resources strategically. For instance, during flu seasons, AI could foresee an influx of patients with respiratory symptoms and prompt hospitals to adjust staff schedules and resource availability accordingly.

The fusion of AI and healthcare resembles the alchemical process (alluded to near the beginning of this chapter), in which raw medical data becomes valuable diagnostic insights. Just as data serves as foundational elements, AI acts as the catalyst, transforming complex data into actionable intelligence. This resonates with my approach to data-driven innovation, in which AI-driven insights empower businesses to make informed decisions. This very easily fits the definition of firepower.

Moreover, the ethical considerations intertwined with AI's ascendancy mirror a guiding ethical compass—an innate sense of responsibility rooted in principles of transparency, fairness, and accountability. Just as ethical governance is paramount in data usage, the judicious wielding of AI is essential. This commitment resonates with the dedication to uphold ethical standards, both in professional pursuits and roles that extend beyond.

Embracing AI tools does not necessarily have to imply an ethical lapse of judgment or lead to a moral dilemma. Using these tools in conjunction with data warehousing, data storytelling, business intelligence, data governance, or data transformation practices should be viewed as a means whereby human ingenuity and creativity are enhanced, not replaced. We must recognize that these fascinating tools are simply that: TOOLS. They are neither good nor evil; they are neither better nor worse than other tools. Using a tool as a crutch leads to over-dependence upon that tool, producing laziness and squelching creativity. However, using that same tool as a lever leads to balance and proper focus, thus becoming a force multiplier. The key to success lies in realizing that you must use the tool; never let the tool use you. A tool is only as good as the hand that wields it and the heart that shields it.

The case study of AI's impact on healthcare underscores the potential of emerging technologies to reshape industries. Just as AI sculpts medical data into diagnostic insights, its integration in various sectors can lead to unprecedented innovation. However, this transformation must always be guided by ethical principles and a clear understanding of AI's role as an enhancement, not a replacement, aligning with the essence of responsible AI integration.

The fusion of AI's transformative potential with a conscientious and ethical approach embodies the essence of the journey through data's realm. As AI shapes insights from data, it reflects the craftsmanship of a sculptor shaping raw material into art. The healthcare example demonstrates how AI's precision revolutionizes diagnosis and treatment, much like a virtuoso sculptor bringing life to a form. By embracing emerging technologies and weaving them with ethical considerations, businesses can create a symphony of innovation, reshaping industries and guiding them toward a harmonious future.

Concluding Thoughts: Data's Illuminating Potential

In the grand tapestry of existence, data radiates a firepower akin to light, illuminating the shadows of ignorance and fostering the brilliance of enlightenment. This metaphor, like the other metaphors explored in this chapter, harmonizes with my resolute mission to "bring data to life," fueling a path that steers others toward the profound potential of data-driven decision-making.

Just as light reveals hidden truths, data unveils insights, exposes intricacies, and ignites innovation. It stands as a torchbearer, leading businesses, and individuals on a triumphant journey toward success. Drawing from my extensive career in IT, data management, and innovation, I dedicate myself to illuminating the path ahead, unveiling clarity amidst complexities and empowering businesses to stride forward with unwavering confidence.

In a 2021 study of more than a thousand technology and business executives, IBM data scientists discovered a startling revelation. Bad data has the potential to cost companies an average of $15 million a day, illustrating the dire consequences of neglecting data quality. Astonishingly, 73% of those surveyed expressed dissatisfaction with their data's accuracy, revealing the pervasive impact of inadequate data management practices. Furthermore, the study found that 61% of the organizations were unable to harness data effectively to establish a sustained competitive advantage. This underscores the importance of not just possessing data, but also understanding, managing, and leveraging it as a potent resource. This very easily fits the definition of firepower.

Real-world anecdotes further emphasize the crucial role of responsible data handling. On September 23, 1999, NASA's Mars Climate Orbiter, intended for a historic orbit insertion around Mars, tragically met its end due to a navigational error rooted in conflicting data units. A seemingly minor oversight in data compatibility (commands sent from Earth in English units while the orbiter expected Metric units) resulted in the incineration of a $125 million spacecraft and set back Martian climate study by years. Similarly, Christopher Columbus's miscalculations in interpreting data led to misconceptions about the distance between Europe and Asia. Columbus favored the values given by Persian geographer Alfraganus, ignoring the more accurate calculations of Greek geographer Eratosthenes. He also mistakenly assumed that Alfraganus referred to Roman miles when he was actually referring to Arabic miles. These stories serve as cautionary tales, highlighting the need for discernment in data interpretation and decision-making.

In the realm of data, two perspectives intertwine: trusting in reliable data and following one's instincts. Just as Columbus's journey was influenced by both accurate and erroneous data, a data strategy must be informed by trustworthy information while also accounting for intuitive judgment. Recognizing the value of accurate data and the dangers of unvetted information empowers us to tackle challenges, create value, and make informed decisions. As we understand the perils of bad data and harness data's firepower to illuminate the path forward, we ensure that our decisions resonate with clarity and purpose, driving us towards a brighter future.

As a torchbearer, I walk in the footsteps of those who paved the way: visionaries who perceived the transformative might, or firepower, of data. Their legacy intertwines with the teachings of my faith, propelling me to guide organizations through the intricate terrain of data, illuminating a trajectory toward a future defined by integrity and the relentless pursuit of progress. This united force of knowledge and belief drives me onward, inspiring organizations to navigate the intricate web of data and embark on a journey shaped by insight, and most importantly, unwavering integrity, as I seek to bring data to life. Following the principles, I outlined in this chapter may not get you credited with saving a Mars Orbiter or helping someone discover a new continent on the other side of the globe (or even find a shortcut to Asia), but you will certainly make some headway in tackling challenges, creating value, making the right kinds of decisions with data, and most of all, bringing it all to life!

Coach MJ's Firepower Takeaways

Data is the modern-day firepower that enables organizations to make informed decisions, innovate, and overcome challenges.

It is essential to harness this power responsibly and ethically, while ensuring that data-driven insights are actionable and aligned with strategic goals.

A robust data warehousing architecture is essential for efficient data delivery, enabling organizations to harness the power of data to make informed decisions and drive innovation.

- Data storytelling is an art that can be used to weave raw information into compelling narratives that captivate and inform decision-makers, leading to transformative outcomes.
- AI's integration in various sectors can lead to unprecedented innovation, revolutionizing industries and guiding them towards a harmonious future, as long as we realize that its role should be clearly understood as an enhancement, not a replacement.
- Responsible data handling is essential for avoiding costly errors and ensuring accurate decision-making.

By recognizing the value of accurate data and the dangers of unvetted information, we can harness data's firepower to illuminate the path forward and drive towards a brighter future.

Thanks, Dr. Joe!

"Unleashing Innovative Mindsets: Revolutionizing Organizational Transformation in the 21st Century through Artificial Intelligence"

Major General (Retired) David Glaser
Chief Strategy Officer

David Glaser, Major General (retired in 2021) and as Chief Strategy Officer at Sam Houston State University (SHSU), stands at the forefront of academic and strategic excellence. His distinguished career spans various leadership roles, including Provost Marshal General for the U.S. Army, Commander of the U.S. Army Criminal Investigations Command, and Senior Advisor to the Ministry of the Interior in Afghanistan. A graduate of prestigious institutions like UNC Kenan-Flagler Business School and Syracuse University, David's expertise extends to international presentations and consultations, covering strategy, leadership development, innovation, crisis management, and security. He's an esteemed member of the FBI National Executive Association and the International Association of Chiefs of Police.

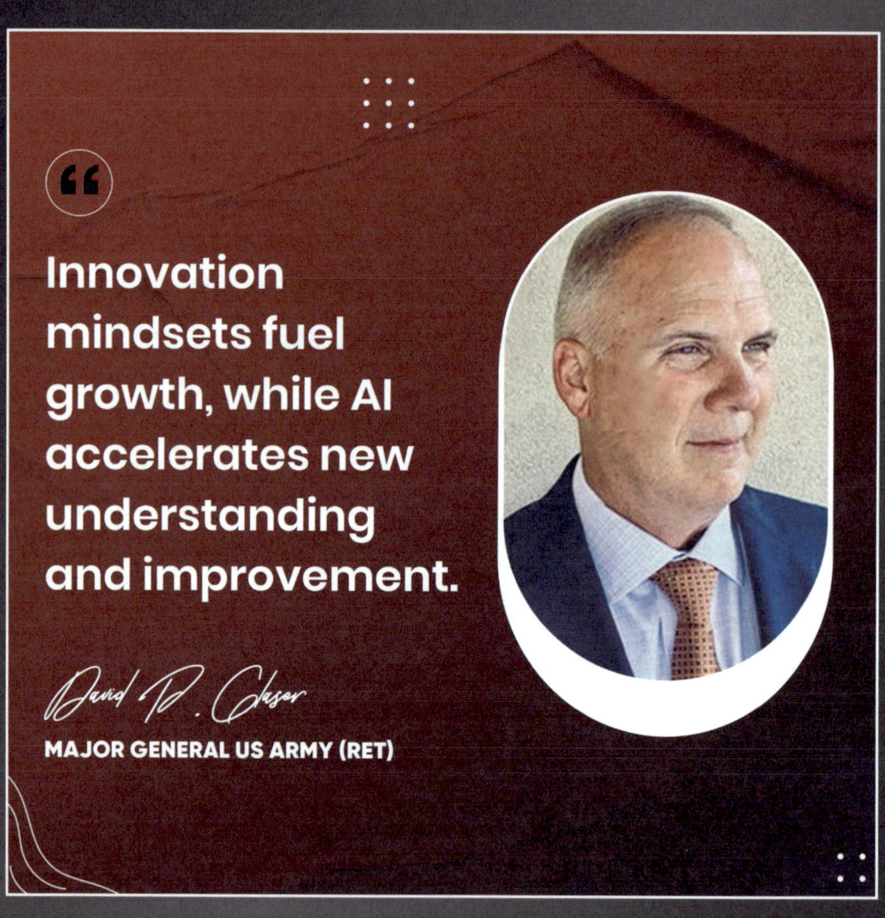

"The universe is change; our life is what our thoughts make it."

MARCUS AURELIUS

I have been blessed to work in and lead organizations (US Army, Think Tanks, Higher Education, Professional Associations, Corporate Advisory Boards, and raise a Family!) that operate in complex, rapidly evolving landscapes, and I've witnessed firsthand the power of transformative thinking. In every instance, the organizations were constantly challenged to adapt, innovate, and stay ahead of the curve. However, the future we face is different; the pace of change is accelerating nearly exponentially as are the tools available to assist our decision-making. To thrive in this dynamic environment, a mere iterative approach is no longer sufficient. The marriage of innovative mindsets and cutting-edge technologies like artificial intelligence (AI) is redefining the possibilities for organizational growth. This chapter explores the intersection of these two vital components—innovative mindsets and AI—and their potential to steer organizations toward unparalleled success in this era of dynamic change.

Unleashing Game-Changing Mindsets

As a former military leader and now a strategist, I understand the significance of an organization's mindset. Traditionally, leadership focused on hierarchical structures, procedural efficiency, and adherence to proven methods. However, in both military operations and the academic realm, I've seen the importance of agility. The innovative mindset shuns rigidity, embracing change as a constant. Just as on the battlefield, where rapid adjustments are vital, organizations must exhibit agility to thrive amidst uncertainties. Agility is borne out and honed through a culture of innovation while both agility and a culture of innovation require trust, diversity, collaboration, and broad context to flourish. Without the organizational foundation described below, all the Artificial Intelligence tools in the world will only make you average or worse.

Embrace a Culture of Teamwork and Innovation

To foster a game-changing mindset, organizations build a culture that celebrates teamwork and innovation at every level. Leaders should encourage cross-institutional partnering and open communication, where employees feel empowered to think broadly and share their ideas without fear of criticism. Regular cross-institutional brainstorming sessions, work groups, and innovation labs can provide platforms for nurturing creativity. IBM's original 15% time (dating to 1948) and Google's "20% time," where employees are encouraged to spend a portion of their work hours on personal projects, are examples of how fostering innovation can lead to groundbreaking ideas. By valuing personal initiative, experimentation, and providing resources for exploring new concepts, organizations can create an environment that fosters a game-changing mindset.

Empower Entrepreneurial Thinking

Encouraging employees to adopt an entrepreneurial mindset such as the ability to take initiative, adapt to change, find creative solutions, and be comfortable with risk can be a game-changer within an organization. This involves granting them autonomy and ownership over their projects, allowing them to take calculated risks and make decisions independently. The startup mindset, characterized by fail-fast experimentation, learning, resilience, and a willingness to pivot, can be harnessed even in large corporations. Companies like Uber, Airbnb, and Amazon have institutionalized this mindset by adopting small team structure (5-8 people), ensuring that teams are small enough to remain nimble and innovative. When individuals take ownership of their roles and are given the freedom to experiment, game-changing ideas are more likely to emerge.

Note: Amazon CEO Jeff Bezos Rule: No meeting should be so large that two pizzas won't feed the whole group

Diversity as a Catalyst

A diverse workforce (life and professional experience, culture, educational background, geographic location, seniority, skills) is a wellspring of innovative ideas. Organizations that prioritize diversity benefit from a variety of perspectives and experiences, which can lead to breakthrough innovations. Different backgrounds and viewpoints challenge conventional thinking and foster creativity. To truly harness the power of diversity, organizations must create environments where every voice is heard and respected. This approach not only brings in fresh ideas but also reflects the varied needs of a global customer base, contributing to a game-changing mindset that aligns with the complexities of the modern interconnected world.

Agile Adaptation to Change

A game-changing mindset thrives on agility—the ability to adapt quickly to changing circumstances. Traditional hierarchical structures can impede the speed of decision-making and innovation. Agile methodologies, as demonstrated by Proctor and Gamble, Apple, and software developers, promote cross-functional collaboration, iterative development, and responsiveness to customer feedback. By adopting agile principles, organizations can break down silos and enhance flexibility, allowing them to seize opportunities and address challenges swiftly. This adaptive approach is essential for staying relevant in today's rapidly evolving markets.

Customer-Centric Focus

Organizations that prioritize customer needs and feedback are more likely to develop products and services that truly resonate. A game-changing mindset necessitates a deep understanding of customer friction points, desires, and behaviors. This requires ongoing engagement through surveys, user testing, and data analysis. Apple, Discount Tire and Proctor and Gamble's customer obsession are prime examples of how this approach can drive innovation. By consistently striving to meet and exceed customer expectations, organizations can create products that disrupt markets and transform industries.

Continuous Learning and Growth

A game-changing mindset requires a commitment to ongoing learning and professional development. Leaders should encourage and reward employees who expand their skill sets and explore new domains, both within and outside their core roles. Learning opportunities, such as workshops, continuing education, and mentorship programs, can inspire fresh perspectives and fuel innovative thinking. Furthermore, organizations should create a culture where employees are encouraged to take risks and learn from their mistakes. The US Army does this through its After-Action Review (AAR) process. AARs are a professional discussion of an event/activity/project that enables Project Teams/units to discover for themselves what happened and develop a strategy for improving performance. They provide candid insights into strengths and weaknesses from various perspectives and feedback and focus directly on the purpose and objectives of the project. This culture of continuous growth can infuse a sense of curiosity, exploration, and most importantly trust into the organization's DNA.

External Collaboration and Ecosystem Building

No organization exists in isolation. Collaborating with external partners, startups, and industry experts allows you to better see yourself and can inject new ideas and approaches. By building a collaborative ecosystem (Customers, Experts, Community leaders, others), organizations can tap into a network of innovation that transcends their internal capabilities.

Organizational incubators, accelerator programs, and partnerships with universities can provide access to cutting-edge research and emerging technologies. This collaborative approach enables organizations to stay at the forefront of industry trends and drive game-changing innovations.

The transition from traditional to innovative mindsets may encounter resistance. Leadership must communicate the rationale behind the transformation, address concerns, and provide necessary training and support to guide their teams effectively. Simultaneously, leaders must understand that the pace of change is accelerating nearly exponentially as are the tools to assist decision-making. To thrive in this dynamic environment, a marriage of innovative mindsets and cutting-edge technologies like artificial intelligence (AI) must take place.

The Emergence of Artificial Intelligence as a Strategic Asset

AI has transformed from a futuristic concept to a pivotal force driving every organization I have been a part of, and all those my kids will be part of in the future. It encompasses technologies such as machine learning, natural language processing, and predictive analytics, offering capabilities to automate tasks, analyze vast datasets, and forecast trends. The successful integration of AI empowers organizations to achieve strategic goals.

- Precision through Data-Driven Insights: Just as strategic decisions in the military require accurate intelligence, organizations today demand data-driven insights. AI processes vast datasets at remarkable speeds, enabling leaders to make informed decisions with unparalleled precision.
- Strategic Planning and Predictive Analysis: In my role as a strategist, I've learned that informed decision-making hinges on predictive

analysis. AI, akin to strategic planning, identifies patterns in data and offers foresight that guides organizational strategies.
- Optimizing Operations and Resource Allocation: AI's role in enhancing efficiency is akin to optimizing resources in a military campaign. By analyzing historical data, AI uncovers operational inefficiencies, guiding organizations to make better use of their resources.
- Enhanced Customer Engagement: AI-driven technologies like chatbots and recommendation systems enhance customer experiences. By analyzing customer behavior, AI tailors' interactions, anticipates needs, and provides personalized solutions, boosting satisfaction and loyalty.

The integration of AI requires careful planning and consideration of ethical implications. Organizations must establish frameworks to mitigate bias, ensure data privacy, and define guidelines for AI's responsible deployment.

The Confluence of Innovative Mindsets and AI: Pioneering Transformation

The fusion of innovative mindsets and AI marks a turning point for organizations. This synergy cultivates a culture of continuous improvement and adaptive innovation. Here's how the interplay between these two elements amplifies their impact:

- Nurturing a Culture of Learning: An innovative mindset is synonymous with continuous learning. AI, driven by its capacity to process vast amounts of information, accelerates learning by extracting insights from extensive data. Organizations can leverage AI to identify emerging trends, anticipate market shifts, and catalyze informed decision-making.
- Elevating Human Potential: The marriage of AI and innovative mindsets redefines roles and reinvigorates human potential. By

automating routine tasks, AI liberates human resources for strategic thinking and creative problem-solving. This transition necessitates upskilling to harness AI's potential optimally.

- Amplifying Innovation: Innovation thrives in environments that foster experimentation and calculated risk-taking. AI's predictive capabilities offer a safety net for innovation. Organizations can leverage AI to simulate scenarios, forecast market reactions, and refine strategies before implementation.
- Personalizing Leadership Development: AI's precision aligns with the innovative mindset required of leaders. It enables tailored leadership development programs by assessing individual strengths, identifying areas for growth, and catering to distinct learning preferences.
- Real-Time Decision-Making: AI's real-time analytics align seamlessly with the agile mindset. Organizations can leverage AI-generated insights to make swift, well-informed decisions—vital in rapidly changing landscapes.

The integration of innovative mindsets and AI is not without challenges. Organizations must address the resistance to change, navigate ethical concerns, and establish effective human-AI collaboration models.

From Strategy to the Board Room: An AI-Driven Odyssey

The remarkable journey of infusing innovative mindsets and AI extends beyond academia and military contexts, finding its place within the corporate realm. As a member of corporate advisory boards, I've witnessed the transformative potential of AI-driven strategies. Organizations, much like strategic military campaigns, require insightful decision-making that anticipates market shifts and ensures long-term success. The dynamic landscape of the boardroom demands agile leadership and calculated risk-taking; qualities synonymous with innovative mindsets. By integrating

AI into corporate strategies, businesses can harness predictive analytics to identify emerging trends, optimize resource allocation, and enhance decision-making. This fusion offers a competitive edge that aligns seamlessly with the strategic demands of the boardroom, ultimately propelling organizations toward enduring success.

Overcoming Challenges and Upholding Ethical Standards

While the fusion of innovative mindsets and AI offers transformational potential, challenges and ethical considerations must be navigated.

- Cultivating Change: Shifting organizational mindsets demands change management, whether in the military, academia, or corporate world. Communication, education, and leading by example are essential to facilitate this transformation.
- The Ethical Imperative: AI's influence must align with ethical considerations. Mitigating bias, ensuring data privacy, and addressing job displacement require organizations to establish ethical frameworks for AI deployment.
- Human-Machine Collaboration: Achieving harmony between AI and human collaboration is crucial. AI augments efficiency, but the human element contributes empathy, judgment, and innovative thinking.

Organizations must embrace a holistic approach, combining training, guidelines, and oversight to ensure AI is used responsibly and ethically.

From Strategy to Academia: An AI-Driven Odyssey

An illustration of the remarkable synergy possible between innovative mindsets and AI unfolds within the realm of academia. As the Chief Strategy Officer at Sam Houston State University, I have the privilege of witnessing firsthand the transformative power of this dynamic partnership.

At Sam Houston State University, we are embarking on an AI-driven journey that will fundamentally reshape how we approach education. Leveraging advanced AI capabilities, we are working to pioneer an innovative approach to student success and learning enhancement. Through the lens of the innovative mindset, we recognize that the one-size-fits-all model of education no longer suffices in a world characterized by diverse learning styles and individual preferences.

By harnessing the analytical prowess of AI, we are analyzing student data in a way that goes beyond traditional assessment methods. The integration of AI technologies will enable us to discern patterns and trends that would otherwise remain obscured. These insights into student behaviors, engagement levels, and learning trajectories will empower us to tailor educational offerings in unprecedented ways.

In the spirit of calculated risk-taking intrinsic to the innovative mindset, we ventured into the realm of personalized learning experiences. By employing AI-driven algorithms, learning paths are being created that are uniquely suited to each student. These paths adapt in real-time based on a student's progress, strengths, and areas that warrant more attention. This approach not only optimizes the learning process but also fosters a sense of individual empowerment and engagement.

One groundbreaking aspect of AI-driven we are working to leverage is an ability to predict academic success with a heightened level of accuracy. By drawing on historical data, behavioral patterns, and academic achievements, AI identifies models that offer insights into students' likelihood of success. Armed with this information, educators can better intervene, providing targeted support to those who may be at risk of falling behind.

The symbiotic relationship between the innovative mindset and AI's capabilities is palpable in our academic endeavors. The innovative mindset propels us to continually push boundaries and explore uncharted territories in education. AI, in turn, facilitates this exploration by providing us with the tools to unlock new avenues of understanding and improvement.

As we navigate this AI-driven odyssey, ethical considerations remain paramount. We are acutely aware of the ethical implications of data privacy, bias mitigation, and the responsible use of AI technologies. This requires the establishment of rigorous protocols and guidelines to ensure that AI-driven initiatives prioritize the well-being and rights of our students.

In the grand tapestry of academia, the fusion of innovative mindsets and AI is redefining the landscape. As we set out on this journey at Sam Houston State University, we do so with a deep-seated commitment to providing an educational experience that embraces diversity, encourages innovation, and harnesses the transformative power of AI to nurture the leaders of tomorrow.

Pioneering Organizational Transformation

In conclusion, the 21st century beckons organizations to embrace innovative mindsets and harness AI's potential. This synergy is not merely a survival strategy but a catalyst for growth. The confluence of AI's analytical prowess and a culture of learning and experimentation holds the power to redefine industries and drive exponential progress.

As organizations embrace this journey, they must address challenges and uphold ethical standards. Effective change management, ethical AI deployment, and seamless human-machine collaboration are integral components of this transformative process.

As we set our sights on the horizon, organizations that foster innovative mindsets while capitalizing on AI's capabilities are poised to excel in the dynamic landscape of the modern world. This transformative journey promises a future where adaptation is continuous, innovation knows no bounds, and leadership evolves in tandem with technology—ushering in an era of unprecedented growth and progress.

Coach MJ's Firepower Takeaways

The Power of the Innovative Mindset: Traditional organizational and leadership models, which often emphasize hierarchy and procedure, are not sufficient for the rapidly changing landscapes of the 21st century.

Embracing agility, fostering a culture of teamwork and innovation, and promoting entrepreneurial thinking within an organization are essential to navigate uncertainties and drive transformation.

Diversity and Adaptability are Key Catalysts for Innovation: A diverse workforce introduces a myriad of perspectives and experiences, which are crucial for fostering creativity and innovative ideas. Additionally, organizations need to prioritize agile methodologies, allowing for quick adaptation to change, breaking down silos, and enabling swift decision-making and innovation.

The Role of AI as a Strategic Asset: Artificial Intelligence (AI) has evolved to be a driving force in organizations, enabling the automation of tasks, extensive data analysis, and trend prediction.

Synergy of Innovative Mindsets and AI: The combination of innovative mindsets and AI leads to a culture of continuous improvement, elevating human potential, enhancing innovation, and promoting real-time, informed decision-making. This relationship aids organizations in continuously pushing boundaries while employing AI to unlock new opportunities for growth and improvement.

Challenges and Ethical Considerations: While the union of innovative mindsets and AI offers numerous benefits, it's essential to address potential resistance to change, navigate ethical issues, and establish effective collaboration models between humans and AI.

Moreover, organizations must prioritize data privacy, mitigate biases, and ensure responsible AI deployment.

Thank you, David!

"Engagement---Your Hidden Superpower"

Kevin Wash

Before becoming a partner at VOS consulting, Kevin Wash led sales teams to produce multi-million-dollar record-breaking achievements of which some of these were within Fortune 500 companies.

His expertise in driving winning sales teams in diverse country markets such as Switzerland, Dubai, South Africa, UK, USA, Spain, Germany, Thailand, Portugal, and more.

He has a tremendous passion for assisting in the growth and development of individuals from both a personal and professional perspective, often taking them to heights they had never believed they were capable of. He has authored several books and appears as a frequent guest on podcasts internationally. Today, he is one of the most sought-after sales trainers in the world.

"Without training, they lacked knowledge. Without knowledge, they lacked confidence. Without confidence, they lacked victory."

JULIUS CAESAR

According to Gallup, the cost of replacing an employee can range from one-half to two times the employee's annual salary. So potentially just in recruitment costs, training, and fees that could be 10's of 1000's of dollars, and then factor in the lost revenue; the cost is horrific.

As a senior trainer and Senior European Board Advisor for Firepower Talent Partners, my role is to enable organizations to tap into higher profitability through enhancing their sales training development programs.

From my own wheelhouse, we offer the power to create the fire to ignite business forward with straight-talking, no-nonsense expert guidance and advice.

Having managed and coached teams that produced multi-million-dollar sales numbers, I offer some new insights here that may seem off-topic from training, but I can assure you they are related.

The topic for this chapter is employee engagement. What does that mean to you and your business--- anything, nothing, something but not too much? Many might not understand the different "levels of engagement" and the impacts of these so allow me to dive in.

What difference would it make to your business if your employees were engaged?

Also, I'm not talking about engagement by letting people finish early one day or dress casually and have free ping pong.

I am talking 100% genuine active engagement as in Phase 2 below.

The 4 Phases of Engagement

1. Engaged
2. Actively Engaged

3. Disengaged
4. Actively Disengaged.

Even in today's uber-commercial world, some things will always surprise me. As external consultants, we are called into companies who are generally looking to increase their revenues, either sales, collections, or sometimes others.

Revenue, we need more revenue, a fairly common shout from the CEO's office, get more revenue. However, sometimes it is not about revenue; it is about efficiency. It is surprising how many companies don't analyze the cost of generating their revenue. The obvious place to look is sales.

Look at the conversions being closed and scream for more. Again, this isn't always the correct answer and not always the best place to look.

Efficiency is the key. If, for example, you have an average sale value of $10,000 and you are converting at 10%, let's keep the math simple. Ten deals per week gives you $100,000 turnover; you increase the closing percentage by 20 to 12% bringing you an extra 2 deals per week and an extra $20,000.

Now look at this if you maintain the same 10% closing but increase your order value by 25% to $12,500, you will achieve higher volumes from the same number of sales and costs, so the logical approach would be increasing your efficiency as in order value first and then start working on ways to increase your closing percentage.

This method will give you success, and it has longevity.

However, what we want to do here is instead of just looking at Sales & Marketing (S&M), let's check the engagement levels of all departments, and let's take a look at the resulting impact of this.

Here are a couple of scenarios you will all be familiar with.

Let us consider two restaurants, with the same quality of food and same price: one has very average service, and the other has excellent, efficient, friendly, and professional service. Which one are you going back to with your leisure money?

Here's another scenario.

You know what it is like when you enter a store; the staff behind the counter ignore you and continue talking to each other.

The result is a lost opportunity for that store, not the individuals.

They are not bad people; they are simply not engaged.

The next store has smiling friendly staff, greeting you at entrance, making you aware they are in place to serve and assist you. I know it is obvious but where will the $'s be spent? Which store? They have the same products, same prices, same offers, just different engagement levels of their team members.

In which stage of the engagement table would you say the staff in these establishments are positioned? I would suggest 2 and 3 possibly; also, both sets of employees are probably paid the same. So, what's the difference?

It is all about the engagement of the staff, direct by-products of increased engagement are the following:

Better client service,
Better responsibility levels,
Higher productivity,
Higher staff retention,
Lower turnover of employees,
Lower costs of annual recruitment and onboarding.

So genuine win-wins all round.

Going back to the cost of recruiting, training, and managing members of sales teams, losing talent is an invisible but significant loss.

This figure very rarely makes it onto the annual Profit and Loss (P&L) forecast and budgets.

It is an absolute crippler as we say in the UK, to your bottom line, and what are you doing to shift the engagement levels, I would venture possibly is not much.

Another common mistake is the way the costs are looked at.

For example, if you invest in Training for Sales and Marketing (S&M) that is fairly easy, you can check the return against the cost very quickly.

Normally with good sales training, you will see an immediate, albeit short-term spike in your revenues, which you can then directly apportion the difference to training costs. Similar lines exist with marketing initiatives and training.

The challenge is how do you measure any impact with non-revenue generating departments?

Most companies have more departments than Sales and Marketing, accounts, collections, administration, reception, client support, presale service, post-sales service, etc. There are many variables.

All of these departments can have a massive impact on how much money a client will spend with you.

It is all about the service and attitude they provide when they "touch" the client. Every contact with a client will impact their perception of your company and its products. The contract will impact significantly on any amount of money the client will spend with you. Poor to average service can result. Maybe they will go for the basic model when the superior one is better suited to them. Good to excellent service will change the sale from the basic to the superior model at no extra cost to your company.

Now here is the scary part. Multiply these 00's of time per year, look at the potential revenues lost, or from another perspective the additional revenues that could be gained from engaged team members.

Let's just look at the table once more.

The 4 Phases of Engagement

1. Engaged: A positive employee who will provide good service levels.
2. Actively Engaged: Super employee who will always get the extra mile, delivering the best.
3. Disengaged: Usually looking for another job, no interest in your clients or product.
4. Actively Disengaged: A dangerous employee, who will try to disrupt team morale and offend clients; this employee will cost you $000's.

You want all your employees in 1 and 2. 3 is a danger sign, and 4 is a virus to remove.

So why is it that so few companies look at the engagement levels of ALL team members?

They will micromanage sales conversion rates, Volume Per Guest (VPG), contact stats, and everything down to the ink they use, and what time of day they talk to people. Sadly, this is only applicable in Sales and Marketing.

So why not use this approach for all departments? Why not just look at engagement levels, nothing else? If you did this, what would your company average be?

Then let's ask the question?

How do you move team members from 3 to 2 and from 2 to 1?
What do you do with the team members at number 4?
How is this impacting your revenues? (Negatively I would guess)

So really by adjusting your cash flow and diverting the replacement costs, converting them into retention investments, and bringing in professional external training to specifically develop and engage your team across all departments, you can make significant increases in revenues.

It is time to stop using that narrow viewfinder and widen the focus from the divas and devils of the S&M departments and bring all employees into your radar screen. It is about appreciating their value and encouraging their personal and professional development. It is not about giving them plaques and flowers. Allow me to expand.

Recently at a company's annual awards ceremony, they gave the top sales performer of the year a brand-new BMW car, the best newcomer of the year (sales) a 2-week cruise plus spending money, salespeople of the month, Plaques, trophies, and cheques of approximately $500.

They then announced a very special award for the longest-serving employee. Her name was Maria; she was one of the drinks ladies, and she had been at the company for 17 years, the longest employee by some distance. They wanted to recognize and thank her for her service and loyalty.

Well, I thought they would possibly fly her family in to present something, also maybe an all-expenses paid 7-night stay in one of the company's luxury properties for her and her family and treat her like royalty. I was actively waiting to see the award and the reactions.

The award she received.
A bouquet of flowers and a plaque.

The ripple effect was that everybody was immediately left with a feeling of low value and worth by the company. If they can treat the longest-serving member like that, how could they possibly care about me? The mood was flattened in one moment; the entire ceremony ended like a damp squib.

Maria resigned the very next day, and really, who could blame her?

What if they had thought this through a bit more, flown her family in, and made her feel special? What would the ripple effect be then?

It would have been priceless, invaluable. You would be running the type of organization that people want to join, want to stay, and aspire in because they recognize the value you placed on every level and department.

Sometimes it is just about the thought, or indeed the lack of it.

Maybe it is time for you to wake up and smell the coffee.

Stop seeing your employees as what they are; see them as who they are and most importantly what they can become.

They are the future of your company, the next generation of leaders, the next CEO.

They will stabilize the workplace.
They will increase retention rates.
They will increase productivity.
They will impact your bottom line.

It is time to invest in your team, your future, before they become somebody else's team and somebody else's future.

When you make the decision to invest in all your departments by bringing in external trainers to inspire, nurture, and drive your team, you embark on the path to forging a bigger, stronger organization with an unbreakable workforce. As you witness astounding improvements across all performance metrics that surpass your wildest expectations, you'll realize the transformation. Whether you lead a company or work within one, it is time to take action and bring about this change.

An engaged team simply becomes an unstoppable force, shattering targets and reshaping the entire workplace. Your pride in your role and your company will soar. Recruitment suddenly becomes effortless, attracting top-tier candidates. A ready-made future management structure will naturally emerge. Clients receive unwavering dedication, with their interests placed above all else. In the end, you will have the luxury to sit back and recognize that your engagement is indeed your hidden superpower while neglecting employee appreciation could prove to be your Achilles' heel.

Coach MJ's Firepower Takeaways

The Cost of Employee Turnover: Replacing an employee can be financially draining for a company, not just in recruitment costs, but also in training expenses and lost revenue. Engagement can help mitigate these costs by promoting staff retention.

The Impact of Employee Engagement on Business: Employee engagement goes beyond superficial benefits like casual dress days. It's about a genuine connection between the employee and the organization.

There are four distinct phases of engagement: Engaged, Actively Engaged, Disengaged, and Actively Disengaged. Shifting employees toward the first two categories can result in better client service, increased responsibility, higher productivity, and reduced turnover.

Efficiency Over Quantity: It's not always about making more sales; it's about the quality and efficiency of those sales. Increasing the value of each sale can be more effective than increasing the number of sales.

Moreover, engagement across all departments can have a massive impact on revenue. Every interaction a client has with any department can influence their perception of a company and affect their buying decisions.

The Real Value of Employee Recognition: Recognizing employee contributions is more than just providing material rewards.

Thoughtful, genuine appreciation can have a profound ripple effect on company morale. Conversely, insincere or inadequate recognition can demoralize and alienate valuable employees, leading to talent loss.

The Power of Genuine Engagement: Investing in all team members and recognizing their potential is essential.

Engaged employees can transform a company, driving productivity, fostering a positive work environment, and ultimately benefiting the bottom line. Leaders should see employees not just for their current roles but for the potential they bring and the future leaders they can become.

In essence, employee engagement is not just a nice-to-have but a crucial superpower that can drive an organization forward, impacting everything from sales efficiency to employee morale. Ignoring or mishandling it can be costly, both in terms of finances and company culture.

Well done, Kevin!

"Teamwork in the Corporate Environment"

James T. Quilley

James has one of the most diverse career backgrounds imaginable. Spanning over 35 years, starting work at an early age, he has risen from the front lines to the pinnacle positions of several industries. Working in 18 countries in the industries of sports, leisure, hospitality, real estate, banking, and management consulting, today he is a sought-after speaker, trainer, and editorial contributor.

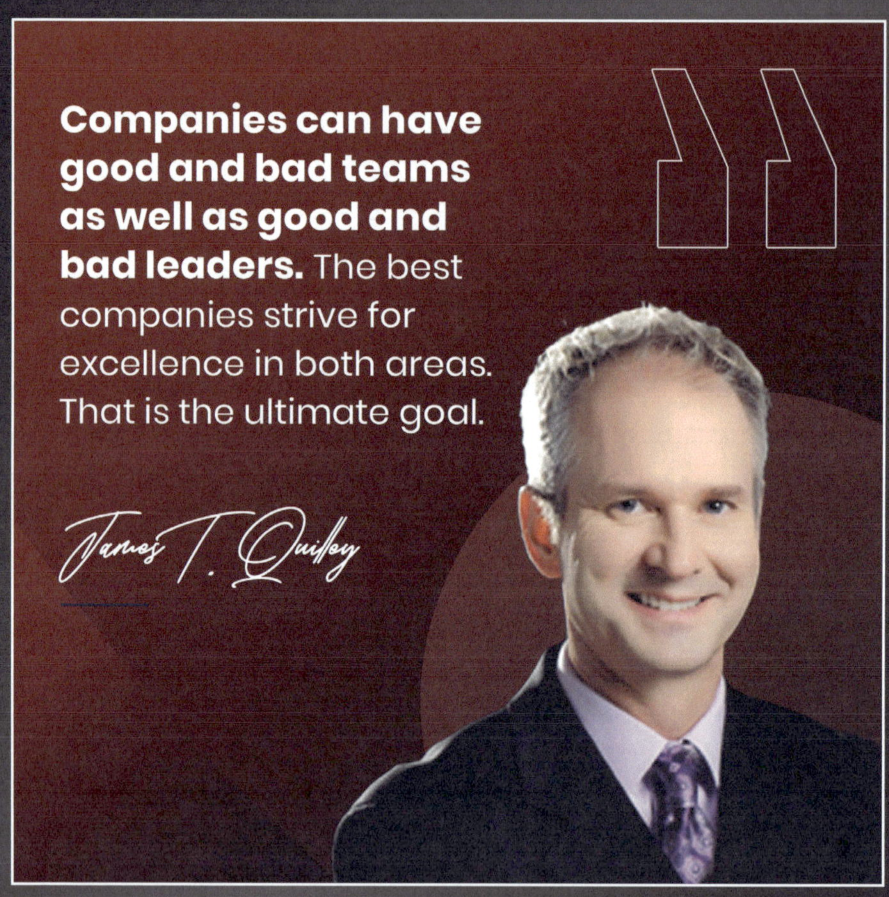

"Harmony is unity in action."

PYTHAGORAS

The word 'Teamwork' is extensively used in business, often advocated by HR staff, and occasionally enforced by organization leaders. Why?

Consider this: Most people in your organization secured their positions through personal competition, self-development, self-motivation, and individual efforts during the recruitment process. Isn't it peculiar that we then welcome new staff to 'the team' by introducing coaching and persuasion to encourage teamwork, collective work, and idea sharing? Granted there are exceptions. Bear with me if you are one of those rare organizations that truly has a team approach established.

The concept of teamwork in the business world fascinates me. I played many team sports in my youth which led me to be fortunate enough to be part of Championship teams. I also experienced gut-wrenching losses on teams that I hated being a part of. I've worked in 18 countries so far with over 200 companies, being employed in every level of position from entry-level to management consultant. Despite differences in national culture, work culture, size of companies, religion, language, company history, highly skilled, educated teams, rookies, and third-world educated teams – there is a common trait I see in teamwork. You feel it when it is present just as you can sense when it is absent. It is what every leader seeks to develop, needs to develop, and maintain; yet there is no textbook, Standard Operating Procedure (SOP), or even hidden secret to "getting it." Or is there? I think I have some solutions.

Let us examine the issue for a moment, dare I say, let us compare our work environments to the sports world for a moment. In the realm of teams (which most businesses inherently are), the most successful teams consistently exhibit shared traits such as respect, commitment, acceptance, utilization of diverse talents, collective discipline, rewards, loyalty, open communication, and clearly defined group goals.

What winning teams do not display is self-preservation, self-focus, confidentiality, segregation; lack of discipline, lack of rewards, unshared goals, selective inclusion, and independence.

So, if this is so obvious in the sports/team world, then why in business when we raise the term or subject of teamwork is it often so strangely different? We tend to rely on analogies about the survival tactics of wild animals, sentimental portrayals of loving families holding hands, and metaphors involving inanimate objects like chains with their weakest links. I'm not dismissing these comparisons; they are all accurate and valid. However, can real, working people truly embrace and absorb them as reality? Posters or messaging in emails are something we've all seen. But are they genuinely catalysts or strategies, or are they simply reflections of the team culture's goals? Most professional sports teams have several inspirational messages, mementos, and devices to celebrate teamwork. These techniques additionally allow the team to display their feelings of pride and purpose, but not all of them are successful. Clearly, there is more to it than that. With that said, let us give the HR department a break and understand that there is a responsibility for everyone within the team to accept and invest themselves in it. It is not solely the leader, HR department, or a few key individuals who are going to "create teamwork."

Let us look at some notable team examples.

- WINNERS the Jamaican Bobsled Team – The incredible formation of a team of guys who came from a position of "no chance," a situation that was perhaps illogical. The challenges they faced were immense and somewhat ridiculous, but what mattered was the dynamics of the team and all those values inherent. They amazingly made it to the Olympics and won the hearts of humanity all over the globe. It is more than just a feel-good story; it is an acute example of the effectiveness of the power of teamwork.

- LOSERS the 1991-92 New York Rangers Hockey Team – acquiring the often-touted greatest hockey leader ever, Mark Messier, a proven record-breaking champion. He could not bring his team to victory. I'm not blaming Mr. Messier. This is an example of "teamwork" leading us back to the point that it takes the whole team, not just a great leader.
- LOSERS the 2003-04 Los Angeles Lakers Basketball Team – despite acquiring a literal powerhouse of talent and leaders. It was evident by the poor performance of the team and ongoing tensions noticed throughout the season that these stars could not work together to a point where in some cases it went as far as not working for the coach/leader.
- WINNERS the 2022-23 Las Vegas Golden Knights Hockey Team – For an ice hockey team to experience immediate, lasting success in a part of the world that is a stranger to ice and winter sports is remarkable. As a blend of veterans and rookies, the team had immediate success at the pinnacle of their league in the Championship Finals; every year, after only 6 years and several outstanding showings, this team achieved the ultimate by winning the League Championship. This particular example, related to business, showcases the power of marketing and public relations, outside the team. As the direct sports team, the players, as well as coaches, had to find that chemistry in order to perfect that winning teamwork formula. However, as the bigger picture business organization, the entire organization embraced the goals and opportunities deemed necessary to create an environment for the players to develop positive feelings reinforcing the confidence, enjoyment, and pride necessary to catalyze their ability to achieve their goals. One could argue that the business team surrounding them played as significant a role in the Golden Knights' success as the players on the ice did.

There are multiple reasons why the LOSERS did not display their "on paper" potential. Likewise, there are multiple reasons why the WINNERS were able to overcome the seemingly insurmountable odds to achieve unusual success. There is one clear answer though – TEAMWORK. It was what was lacking with the losers additionally, it was what was abundant with the winners.

I'll share with you a couple of direct work experiences of teamwork success.

The most enjoyable and successful chapter in my career was while working with a company named International Management Group (IMG). At its core, it is a sports business company, the foundation of which was built on working with athletes through representing them in endorsement deals and contracts. What struck me about this role was that everyone I worked with had a common interest in sports, whether a fan or a player of various sports; everyone had a common passion for sports in general, and that showed on a daily basis. Conversation in the workplace would often alternate from work tasks to personal hobbies rather effortlessly. It felt like an incredibly special workplace even though most IMG employees did not ever meet the celebrity sports figures that were our clients. We could all relate to the photos on our office walls and connect when seeing them on TV at home or on billboards within our city or abroad on our travels. We always felt a connection and a greater sense of purpose, vs. just going into an office to begin doing assigned tasks or producing administrative records or documents for someone else, which may very indirectly actually have something to do with that industry of sports stars.

Nevertheless, we celebrated this, and all enjoyed a chance to chat about sports where the team was able to share stories of what we saw and read all together about the sports stars. We also found enjoyment in our local clubs as we gloated about beating the neighborhood team at our favorite activity. This subtle bond was a powerful catalyst for us all to work together in harmonious enjoyable ways deemed to be highly effective.

I've always said I never felt that anyone was a clock watcher or lagging in pulling their weight, rather it was enjoyably noticeable that anyone from the office, whether it was the Finance Manager to the Janitor, or the "guy across the hall," would be willing to jump into a spontaneous meeting to collaborate, help another colleague work or personal, stay late, come early, do something in someone else's department, and generally contribute to the greater cause of the regional office.

I would say this was the informal formation of a team, which we joined without even being aware of at the time of hiring. Focused recruiting? Luck?

Let me quickly address that last point in another example of a great work experience I enjoyed while working for 7 years with a company called Sun Peaks Resort. It was traditionally a ski resort but expanded into other seasons and activities. Nevertheless, the history and core atmosphere would always remain, predominantly, a ski destination. It all started with recruiting. It was mandatory, a prerequisite, that every new hire had to enjoy skiing. This was debated (perhaps politely protested…) by many managers, looking for simply the best technical staff in their required roles; however, it was unwaveringly communicated that this was non-negotiable. Locate a suitable candidate who possesses a genuine enthusiasm for skiing. The only exceptions I remember involved new hires who persuasively expressed their eagerness to learn to ski despite never having had the opportunity to try it before. They followed through without any problems. What a fantastic result this had. The shared, common bond was the same as what I explained earlier within the IMG world of sports. People would always comment on the snow conditions, the temperature, the snow quality, ski events, not only ours but globally, whatever was on TV – World Cups, Olympics, etc. This common thread amongst us led to ease, acceptance, and a bond that made communication along with engaging with one another second nature. We all felt able to approach one another at any time for any issue no matter how big or small or outside of anyone's wheelhouse because we felt a part of something bigger that we were all fabricated into.

For comparison's sake, so you don't think I've had a joyous, uneventful career, let me quickly share a challenging situation with a silver lining. I was part of a small team—five of us—responsible for running operations in a small, customer-facing business generating about 2 million dollars in annual revenue. Our office was always bustling. Unfortunately, our leader was incompetent, a fact we all unanimously agreed upon. He was cold, distant, unpredictable, somewhat arrogant, and perpetually too busy to engage in conversations, provide coaching, or make decisions. We were never sure if he was 'in' or 'out.' Among ourselves, we often vented our frustrations about him, blaming him for all our challenges and setbacks until one day, one of our team members took the lead.

They said, 'This is toxic, we all want to quit, but why should we? We can do what we want, and he won't even notice. So why don't we just run this place the way we know it should be?' We then took two significant actions. Firstly, we created a money jar, created a diary for daily communication every time, and scheduled regular meetings for expressing concerns and devising solutions. Our boss eventually stumbled upon the money jar and explained to our customers that it was a penalty for each mistake, for which we were accountable. He also became aware of our diary and meetings, surprisingly offering unexpected compliments and acknowledging their value.

Despite occasional conflicts with him, we essentially presented an ultimatum: if we weren't allowed to do things our way, we would all resign. Mutiny? Perhaps. Regardless, it serves as a compelling example of thriving teamwork in the face of extremely poor leadership. So, does this imply that leadership is irrelevant? No. However, it does emphasize the distinction between the two. Companies can have good and bad teams as well as good and bad leaders. The best companies strive for excellence in both areas. That is the ultimate goal.

So how do you create Teamwork if you are the CEO or in a position where you feel you should create this, either overall, for the whole organization or in a smaller fraction of a bigger organization?

My experience leads me to believe this.

- Starting Point: Whether you have a new team, a new company, or are joining a mature established group if you're aiming to develop or enhance teamwork, a reset and a clear statement are essential. Ensure that everyone recognizes the need for a fresh start. Hold a mandatory company-wide meeting. Temporarily suspend business operations for one or two days. It is crucial. The message must sternly convey that this is of utmost importance. It will be worth it.
- Establish the Leader: This may seem obvious, but I've seen CEOs who hire someone to execute this for them while they sit off to the side. They then re-surface afterwards in company memos and meetings, as if they are the team leader, but I've never seen this being embraced by a team. This does not work. You don't need to step down as CEO, but whoever you appoint should be readily available and responsible for overseeing the outcomes regarding the future of the teamwork culture thereafter. Think of it as establishing a Coach vs. a GM. If you only require a facilitator, they should not speak for more than 30% of the time, with the remaining 70% handled by the 'coach/leader.'
- Include Everyone: Impractical as this may seem, it is easier now than ever with video group calls and large video monitors. More effective in person, but at least get everyone in on the discussion, right from the start. This is very important.
- Develop your Own Language: Do not try to create profound slogans or technical words or borrow from some great philosophers or accomplished executives. Use the common language that is

emanating from within the team. Use your employee's comments. This will resonate with the team in the future. They are writing their vision and their destiny. It becomes compelling.

- Establish Goals and Standards: Maybe you need a new Vision or Mission Statement. Maybe you just need to update an existing one but go through and examine what you have right from the essence of the company existing. There are at least 7 key, critical questions that you need to raise and answer together as a team.
- Map out the day-to-day: What is on the agenda for tomorrow? You must provide a detailed plan, breaking it down from the high-level perspective to the team's level. Think of it as Offense and Defense Teams, each with distinct strategies, roles, in addition to tasks, but they are all integral members of the larger team. It is crucial for them to communicate, support one another, as well as remain connected in order to secure victory.
- Create a Scoreboard: Imagine a team participating in game after game, never knowing if they scored, won, or lost, or where they stand in the league. Astonishingly, this represents a significant gap in the teamwork-building process for most organizations. Since it is not a sports game, leaders often overlook this crucial aspect. Measures and outcomes must be shared to generate momentum; thus, better sustaining interest and efforts.
- Team Interactions: This is more complex, but anything you can bring to the team(s) to make their work more interesting and foster connections in unique ways will create bonds within the team. Establish a wall of fame in the company offices, transforming it into a timeline by incorporating success "scores" along the way to illustrate that the vision is becoming a reality, with team participation closely tied to it.
- Stick to your Promises: Allowing poor performance to persist is detrimental, having similar consequences to neglecting to reward top performers. In the real world, there are winners and losers.

Demonstrating your commitment to taking everyone's input and commitments seriously, and being willing to enforce discipline, terminate, compensate, or promote is essential. Address situations promptly, without exceptions or hesitations. In the sports world, trades, releases, and acquisitions are routine and embraced. It is no easier for athletes than for employees, but many companies often hesitate to deal with poor performers due to concerns about legal action, financial penalties, or compassion.

- Balance: Intense teamwork is great, nevertheless, tense teamwork is suffocating as it leads to the inability of people to thrive. Incorporate barometers or rest breaks, where you seriously take "time outs" to talk authentically, genuinely as a team among various teams. This demonstrates care, compassion, and sanity. It is necessary.

In summation, successful Teamwork is critical for achieving peak Firepower performance. Its dynamics vary in each team, fluctuating over time. The principles and strategies presented here are proven across diverse cultures, ages, experience levels, genders, and religions. Know this for sure – no great team was ever the result of one individual, whether the owner, coach, superstar performer, or dynamic personality. It is always a combination of different contributions. That is why the processes mentioned are critical to crafting the chemistry found in each true high-performing team. The recipe is proven; what can change is some of the ingredients, the flavors, the cooking times… if you can relate to that analogy. There are a lot of gaps in the solutions I have provided here. It is purposeful. You need to customize the "work" and the details to suit your situation. If you are not sure how or what, ask for help. This is vital to your future survival along with your success.

While great teams may look a bit different in their moments of triumph, even along the journey, the core principles of building strong teamwork remain consistent.

Coach MJ's Firepower Takeaways

Individual vs. Team Paradox:

We hire stars, then ask them to shine together. The shift from solo success to collective effort is complex and calls for finesse.

Sporting Wisdom: Winning sports teams teach us vital lessons about cohesion, shared goals, and leveraging diverse talents. Play the business game like a championship team.

Bonding Beyond Work: Shared passions, like sports, naturally unify teams.

Companies like IMG and Sun Peaks Resort thrive on these common interests, turning workplaces into camaraderie hubs.

Blueprint for Team Triumph: Start fresh, lead clearly, include all, speak a team-tailored language, and keep score. It's teamwork's recipe for success.

The Harmony of Intensity and Ease: Boost teamwork but don't smother. Blend hard-hitting team goals with breezy breaks for genuine connections and peak performance. Balance is brilliance.

Thank you, James!

"Unleashing Firepower for Business: Best Practices from the Battlefield to the Boardroom"

Joe Polanin, Captain

U.S. Navy (retired) Founder and CEO, The Alaka'i Leadership Group

Captain Joseph Polanin, U.S. Navy (retired) is an award-winning CEO and a disabled Navy combat Veteran who served three decades leading elite teams to succeed on complex missions in high-risk environments despite every obstacle.

He has 20+ years as a successful Commanding Officer, Task Force Commander, and Director of Operations (CEO/COO) for globally integrated organizations, led several lasting enterprise transformations, and founded The Alaka'i Leadership Group, LLC, a Strategic Accelerator providing unmatched fractional C-Suite leadership in 2020.

"A leader is best when people barely know he exists, when his work is done, his aim fulfilled, they will say: we did it ourselves."

LAO TZU

Vision, strategy, and talent are three interdependent pillars of excellence that must align seamlessly and evolve in harmony because they form the foundation of phenomenally successful teams, organizations, and companies.

- Vision: A bold expression of an ambitious, seemingly impossible goal that is powerful, is inspirational to others, and communicated consistently well.
- Strategy: A simple, clear, and concise plan of action and milestones. When implemented with precision and accuracy, it will deliver a compelling roadmap to achieve the shared vision. This is the catalyst for a team's success, like an engine driving them forward.
- Talent: People are the heart of every profession and an invaluable capability. Those whom great leaders serve will move mountains when they know their leader cares for them, when they are inspired, and when they are trusted.

Once leaders at all levels in the chain of command understand and appreciate this foundation, they must commit to being ardent students and practitioners of leadership daily. Our talented people deserve nothing less than the absolute best leaders we can become. Great leadership is like a muscle, which needs consistent stress, training, sets and repetitions under a variety of conditions to become stronger and more resilient. Just like physical training and exercise, becoming an inspirational leader requires several critical processes, and there is no simple solution or secret formula. However, all genuinely great leaders share common attributes. They learn to follow first, then they learn to lead themselves, and finally they earn the privilege to lead others and enhance their leadership relentlessly. There are several proven rules, principles, and values that great leaders share, which we will expand upon further.

The 11 Rules of Leadership

Many ask if great leadership is inherited or learned behavior. I believe it is both. Leaders are indeed born, and they are made better through learning, practice, and trial. It is not possible to condense the principles of superior leadership into a single document nor is such a document conceivable. However, it is possible to share best practices and lessons learned to advance collective understanding and application. These 11 Rules were distilled from 30 years of successful military service, 20+ years in Command or CEO/COO equivalent positions. They comprise what worked well and what did not. I believe they are lessons for life that apply universally in every industry and sector.

Rule 1: Leaders Care About People

The best leaders always demonstrate how much they care about people, the heart of every profession. Individual imagination, grit, and the indomitable human spirit outweigh even the most advanced technology. If you are a Founder, CEO, President, Managing Partner, Innovator, Disruptor, or aspiring business leader, then you have a bold vision for the future, which you share powerfully with your team.

Rule 2: Great Leaders Can't Be Mass Produced Quickly

Why not? Because you cannot wait until after a crisis occurs to find bold, talented, and experienced leaders to solve complex and unprecedented problems. You must anticipate those problems before they occur; learning to lead well – especially in a crisis – takes time.

Rule 3: Great Leaders Are Selfless

They always place the needs of others before their own needs in business and in life. Helping your team solve a complex problem, volunteering in your community, caring for the sick, and giving your time and talents to help the hungry and the homeless are the hallmarks of selfless leadership.

Rule 4: Leadership is Not a Position

Great leaders are not defined by a job, a title, or an office. They are not made by wealth, fame, or popularity. Leadership is a process of learning and relentless curiosity — a continuous journey, an evolution, not a destination. Anyone who commits to this approach can be a leader.

Rule 5: Leaders Win

Leaders choose faith over fear: a boundless faith in their vision and their mission and in those whom they serve. Leaders perpetuate a culture of success across their teams. They do not fear failure; they only fear failure to try. Great leaders always have elevated expectations, set seemingly impossible goals, achieve them, and then aim higher. They are relentless in their pursuit of excellence, but they do not seek perfection. In all they do, the best leaders inspire impact.

Rule 6: Leaders Thrive on Change

Successful leaders inspire a culture of innovation across their teams. They empower all around them to be comfortable in uncomfortable, stressful, or crisis situations. "Keep calm and carry on." When others see uncertainty, problems, or roadblocks to success, leaders see opportunities to excel. They have seemingly infinite energy, enthusiasm, and optimism, but they use good judgment and know when to exercise caution.

Rule 7: Great Leaders Inspire Confidence

"Inaction breeds doubt and fear. Action breeds confidence and courage."
- Dale Carnegie

Leaders are self-assured and self-aware. They understand and admit their own strengths and weaknesses. Great leaders inspire confidence among those whom they serve. They overcome fear with action. They are humble. They are neither doubtful nor arrogant. They lead with heart. They are catalysts who ensure others exceed their own perceived limitations or expectations.

Rule 8: Leaders are Quiet Professionals

Leaders get the job done right, the first time, every time. Then, they set to work on the next objective. They do not seek credit or praise. Rather, they downplay their personal contributions to mission success. Great leaders are satisfied only when the achievements of those whom they serve are recognized.

Rule 9: Leaders Ask Insightful Questions

Leaders are curious. They seek the truth. They ask who, what, why, and how? They ask how they can help you, and then they do. They ask the best questions that inspire dialogue and evoke multiple responses.

Rule 10: Great Leaders Forgive

"Forgiveness is not an occasional act; it is a constant attitude."
~ Martin Luther King Jr.

Wherever there is greatness - great leadership, great organization, or even strong emotion - also the potential for error is great. Leaders forgive others, they forgive themselves, and they learn from their mistakes. Exceptional leaders and those they serve will make well-intentioned errors that have consequences. Their ability to forgive honest mistakes and to be compassionate with those whom they serve must remain true, especially in the toughest situations. The crucible of a crisis magnifies a leader's good and bad qualities and demands the highest degree of empathy and forgiveness through which the best leaders emerge.

Rule 11: The Best Leaders Always Do the Right Thing

Leaders do the right thing because they have a deep sense of personal morality. This is not a matter of law or policy. It is a matter of conscience firmly grounded in their code of ethics. The right thing might be the hardest option, but for a leader it is an easy choice.

Founders, CEOs, Presidents, Partners, Innovators, Disruptors, and Future Leaders:

What follows are critically important questions that leaders should ask of themselves and those whom they serve on a recurring basis. Derived from the 11 Rules and practiced successfully in dozens of high-performance organizations, they keep us sharp, focused, and resilient while accelerating our teams' success. I have found the question-and-answer process also inspires leaders to sustain a lifestyle of continuous improvement. It is equally powerful in educating new leaders, beginning innovative ventures, and accelerating established businesses in any stage of organizational development. Please employ them as you deem appropriate.

- What is your plan of action to achieve your shared vision?
- How do you inspire your talented people to embrace the vision and participate in the plan with urgency?
- How do you empower and inspire the leaders you are developing to exceed your expectations and their own perceived potential, thus preparing them for success in future crises?
- How do you demonstrate and inspire selfless leadership across your senior team and your enterprise?
- How do you inspire a culture of curiosity across your enterprise and develop leaders on your team who are lifelong learners?
- How do you inspire, impact and ensure a winning culture across your enterprise?
- How do you inspire a culture of change leadership across your organization?
- How do you inspire confidence among your team to become better than the best leaders you have known?
- How do you lead through action and personal examples?
- How do you demonstrate and inspire quiet professionalism across your organization?
- How do you inspire curiosity across your teams?
- How well and how often do you forgive others and yourself?
- What is your ethical code?

The Principles of Winning Operations

Why are high performing teams and elite organizations persistently successful? Because they have a bold, shared vision, a clear and simple strategy to achieve the vision, and their talented people know they are valued, empowered, and trusted. In short, they are inspired to exceed expectations.

There must be more, right? What other characteristics and capabilities make them successful repeatedly? They focus their efforts precisely and accurately across three lines of effort simultaneously:

- Strategic — the big picture, the long view, the end results desired; the bold vision the team will achieve together
- Operational — the gritty, often unglamorous, and arduous work necessary to integrate all functions and leaders across the organization seamlessly so the team moves forward together in harmony, achieving unity of effort
- Tactical — delivering unmatched excellence to your customers, those whom you serve, and improving the quality of your internal processes daily

Whether you have been an operator for many years or are just getting started in your new profession, congratulations! The Principles of Winning Operations, honed over decades of successful military operations with elite teams in high-risk environments, when applied with resolve, consistency, and discipline, reinforce the positive impact each one of us can have on a winning team.

"If I had something important to tell you,
I would have already told you."
- Joe Polanin, 2002

The First Principle is Communication. Great operators ask themselves these questions persistently and communicate with their teammates openly.

- What critical information do I know? Who else on my team needs to know?
- Have I told them? How did they respond?
- What do we need to do now?

This individual and collective commitment to transparency and caring reinforces mutual respect, builds trust, and forms a lasting culture of open, honest, and candid collaboration on high performing teams. When you care about your people, and you care about your mission, you want to communicate with them. You want to listen, learn, and lead.

"Character is fate." Heraclitus

The Second Principle is Honor. Some know this as integrity. Others call it character, honesty, or an ethical code. For great operators, it is in their DNA. Their actions are forged in honor. They do what is right because it is right. They do the right thing even when no one is looking. They possess the moral courage to admit their own mistakes, and they ensure their teammates thrive in an environment where they can also share their failures freely without fear.

"The only problem I can't help you solve
is the one I don't know about."
- Joe Polanin, 2004

The Third Principle is Support. Just like a family, teams of great operators back each other up. Our support is unconditional. The foundation of mutual support is respect, and mutual respect breed's trust. With trust, we place our very lives in our teammates' hands just as they do in ours. We are there for each other all day, every day, without question or hesitation. This is mission essential. There are too many variables beyond our control for anyone to handle alone. No matter how senior, seasoned, or experienced we are, we all make well-intentioned mistakes. We value, respect, and trust our teammates' insight and intuition especially when they point out our errors.

"Uncomfortable is the new comfortable."
- Joe Polanin, 2021

The Fourth Principle is Curiosity. Chaos, uncertainty, and stress are always with us. They make us stronger. Within these arenas, great operators thrive. We cannot change these conditions. But we can adjust our attitude. Keep calm and carry on is our ethos. We value grit and resilience. We do not make hasty assumptions, especially during a crisis. We rely on facts. If the information we receive does not make sense, we ask questions. If a process is not working, then we ask why not, and we fix it together as a team. If we need to deviate from an established procedure or policy, we understand the prudent risk that may be necessary, and we take that risk together. We must be experts in our profession. We are lifelong learners, and we strive to be the best in our tradecraft.

"Demonstrate that you care."
- Joe Polanin, 2008

The Fifth Principle is Caring. Just like a family, selfless teams of great operators demonstrate that they care for one another, and those whom they serve. Writing about this or talking about it is not enough. You must demonstrate caring through your actions, every day. Genuine caring and compassion are inherited in great operators' DNA, forged within their core values, navigated by their moral compass, and demonstrated over years of action together in serving others. Empathy is an outcome of caring. Great operators have the courage to place the needs of their teammates before their own and in so doing display empathy. This makes the team stronger, more resilient, and capable of overcoming any obstacle together. We respect the seriousness of our duties, responsibilities, and obligations. Empathy allows us to forge unbreakable bonds of trust during the toughest operations and most challenging crises.

Founders, CEOs, Presidents, Partners, Innovators, Disruptors, and Future Leaders:

Remember, operational leadership is the gritty, often unglamorous, and arduous work necessary to integrate all functions and leaders across the organization who move forward together in harmony, achieving unity of effort. It synthesizes your strategy with your tactics. Great operators do this every day because it is who they are. Great operators lead with conviction and serve with honor.

The Leader's Triad: Responsibility, Accountability, Authority

Responsibility, authority, and accountability (or influence) are interconnected and interdependent. The best leaders understand these eternal attributes are inseparable from their unique and inspirational roles. They know their core values, their character, and the position they hold are the same. In all they do, they are genuine and authentic.

Leaders have the duty, indeed the responsibility, to develop their teams to become better than the best they ever knew. That is how the teams evolve together and move forward. That is how the teams tackle the complex problems of tomorrow and innovate beyond the imagination of today. They are responsible to themselves to do what is right; they are responsible to their teams to lead them with integrity; and they are responsible to their organizations to achieve their shared vision together.

Leaders have ultimate accountability for the people under their charge and for accomplishing their mission. When the team succeeds, the leader downplays their contributions and is satisfied only when teammates are recognized publicly for their superior efforts. When any member of the team stumbles or fails in a well-intentioned effort, the leader rapidly takes the blame. The team wins together, but only the leader fails.

Authority (or influence) is not a position, title, or office. It is not about giving orders. Leaders can do that, but that is ineffective and short sighted. Authority is the mandate to inspire and empower people and teams to exceed their potential and expectations---to elevate empathy, respect, and trust and to listen, learn, and create impact for others. Authority means inspiring people to lead meaningful change that lasts. It means serving those whom they lead, and in all things putting their people first. It means sustaining a culture of excellence. Borrowing from Thomas Jefferson, great leaders' authority is for their people.

One person, one leader, can make a tremendous difference for every team and generate untold positive impact for others. However, what a team can accomplish together will always be more important than what anyone can do alone. The best leaders know this, and they serve tirelessly as catalysts for their teams by mobilizing their collective intuition, heart, spirit, and courage toward the team's shared vision.

Coach MJ's Firepower Takeaways

Triple Pillars of Triumph: Vision, strategy, and talent are the intertwined trio underpinning legendary teams. They're the rhythm, lyrics, and melody in the symphony of success.

Leadership Lore: Dive deep into the 11 rules etched from war rooms to boardrooms. A blend of nurture and nature, leadership is an evolving dance where care and selflessness take center stage.

Operational Acumen: For high-fliers, the battlefield is both strategic foresight and gritty groundwork. Remember, a visionary view, operational cohesion, and tactical brilliance are your tickets to eternal excellence.

Operator's Ethos: Communication, Honor, Support, Curiosity, and Caring—these five principles aren't just words. They're the DNA of elite operators, the unseen code propelling world-class teams to glory.

Leader's Sacred Triad: Navigating the leadership labyrinth? Anchor yourself in the holy trinity of Responsibility, Accountability, and Authority. As catalysts, leaders are the magic elixir, empowering teams to chase and catch the stars.

Thank you, Joseph, this was amazing!

"How to Be a Business Rockstar (through Branding and Speaking)"

Dave Crane

Dave's an acclaimed award-winning motivational speaker and CEO mentor, has a 40-year career marked by collaborations with top-tier global brands, leaders, and entertainment icons. Dave's touched over a billion lives as an event facilitator and host of notable sporting and entertainment events. An NLP master practitioner and certified hypnotherapist, Dave's commitment to personal development is evident in his Industry Icon mentoring program, mastermind groups, and The Game Changers community. He is a dynamic presence in the international public speaking circuit and has delivered keynote speeches at prestigious events like NASA and TEDx.

"Courage is what it takes to stand up and speak; courage is also what it takes to sit down and listen."

WINSTON CHURCHILL

Introduction: The New Age of Leadership

In a world filled with change, innovation, and uncertainty, the role of the business leader has evolved into something more profound, influential, and impactful. We have moved beyond the traditional definitions and embraced a new era where CEOs, business owners, and decision-makers are the architects of the future.

The New Titans of Industry: Why Today's Business Leaders are Much More than CEOs

When we think of CEOs, what comes to mind? Corner offices? Suits and ties? Well, scrap that old vision because the role of today's CEOs is akin to being a rockstar—complete with fans, world tours, and the heavy burden of legacy. These are the New Titans of Industry, the game changers who have gone beyond the spreadsheets and into the realm of cultural icons.

Let us look at some real-world rockstars who do not have the guise of CEOs. Elon Musk, anyone? This man is not just about the zoom-zoom of Tesla's electric cars. He is also the visionary orchestrating the "Moonwalk"—and I mean that literally—with SpaceX's incredible forays into space exploration. And how about Satya Nadella? The guy's basically the maestro of a technology symphony at Microsoft, transforming a once stagnant tech behemoth into a nimble, cloud-dancing giant. These are not just CEOs; they are influencers, visionaries, the gods of change.

These titans are doing something most of us only dream of. They are literally reshaping the world! When they strum that guitar or pound those drums—be it launching a new electric vehicle or reviving a company's culture—they do it with a flair that captivates us all.

But here is the kicker! This surging influence is not just a cosmic responsibility descending upon their suited shoulders; it is a golden opportunity. An invitation to step into the spotlight and shred a solo that echoes through eternity. It is a chance to guide, inspire, and craft a legacy that will be sung about long after they have left the stage. We are not just talking profits and loss statements here; we are talking about etching their ethos into the annals of history, making sure their influence is felt not just in quarterly reports but in the very fabric of society.

Think about it. We hang on to their every tweet, parse through their interviews, and dissect their strategies. Why? Because we want a piece of that magic. We follow these leaders into the trenches—sometimes literally if you are tagging along with Elon Musk to Mars! We do not just follow; we mimic, adapt, improvise. We take their proven strategies and adapt them to our own set-lists, looking to replicate their chart-topping hits in our own lives and businesses.

And why should this matter to you?

Well, here is where it gets really fun. You do not have to be an Elon Musk or a Satya Nadella to create transformative waves. Whether you are leading a tech start-up or spearheading social change, you have your own set-list to play. Let us make one thing clear: it is not just about stock prices or mergers. It is about the lives you touch, the minds you inspire, and the world you make better.

So how do you join this legendary league?

Start with vision, add a dash of innovation, and stir in some audacity, and there you have it—a cocktail of greatness. But remember, even the best needs a mentor, a guiding light, someone who has been on that stage before and knows how to work the crowd. That is why mentorship programs like Industry Icon are not just add-ons; they are essential gear in your rockstar toolkit.

So, are you ready to step up? Ready to not just be a leader but a game changer, an influencer, a New Titan of Industry? Well, the stage is set, my friend. The crowd's buzzing; the spotlight's on you. Grab that mic, step into the spotlight, and let us give them a show they will never forget!

When we follow these leaders into battle, we can also mimic their strategies to grow our own successes.

Unleashing Your Inner Icon: The Immeasurable Impact of Crafting a Personal Brand

Now, let us dive into the game-changing world of personal branding. Now, I do not mean just slapping a cool logo on your business card. I am talking about setting the stage on fire with who you are—your values, your vision, your vibe. Ever wonder why legends like Richard Branson and Oprah Winfrey resonate with millions? It is because they have turned themselves into not just brands but icons.

Believe it or not, you can do it, too!

Take Richard Branson, for instance. The guy's a master at making you feel like a rockstar even when you are just boarding one of his Virgin flights. His brand? It is all about innovation and treating customers like royalty. Then we have the Queen of All Media, Oprah Winfrey. She is not just about television; she is a life coach, a philanthropist, a global beacon of empowerment and education.

You see, your personal brand is not just a trendy slogan or a flashy logo. Nope, it is like that golden microphone in your hand, capturing your leadership tone, style, and, of course, your essence. It is your signature tune—the music that people recognize even before they see you coming onto the stage.

But you also must be able to hit the right chords to trust and the credibility to make great business music.

So, why should you care about building this superstar persona?

Well, here is the magic: A dynamite personal brand does not just elevate you; it lifts everyone around you. Your staff, those hard-working heroes backstage, will trust you more. They will see your passion, your commitment, and your vision, and they will want to be a part of that blockbuster tour you are planning.

Now, let us talk about your fans—the clients, shareholders, and suppliers. When they know what you stand for, when they feel the pulse of your brand, they will dance to your tunes and sing along with every word. They are not just buying a product or service; they are buying into a world you have created a world they want to belong to. Let us not forget your shareholders; they are your ultimate groupies. A solid personal brand can be the guitar riff that resonates with them, bonding them to you and your vision.

Have you ever seen a live concert where the best part is the encore? Well, in business terms, that is also your lasting legacy---your standing ovation.

When you build an iconic brand, you are not just leaving a mark; you are etching your ethos into the stars. Long after the concert lights have dimmed and the crowd has dispersed, your impact will continue to ripple through the industries, communities, and lives you have touched.

Excited? Good.

So, I know you are thinking… How do you do this?

How do you become the next chart-topper in your industry? Simple! Identify your passion, crystallize your vision, and communicate it with the kind of flair that makes even the skeptics take notice. And hey, you do not have to go at it alone. Thought Leader Accelerators that are linked to my Industry Icon Program are designed to guide you in tuning your personal brand to perfection.

So, what is stopping you? Grab that golden mic, step into the spotlight, and let the world hear your unique tune. Your journey from a leader to an Industry Icon starts now.

The success stories you create have a knock-on effect everywhere you go in real time, too.

A robust personal brand fosters trust among staff, builds relationships with clients and suppliers, and bonds shareholders.

Your brand is not just your company's logo; it is your leadership signature.

The Symphony of Success: Why Collaboration and Community are Your Secret Weapons

This is not just about brainstorming sessions and teamwork; it is about creating a tribe, a family, a movement! Trust me, the journey from being a solo artist to leading a global band of game-changers is the ultimate thrill ride.

You know, it was this craving for meaningful connection among leaders that sparked the creation of the Industry Icon program and The Game Changers. Let me clarify that this was never just about mentorship. Nope, this is Rock 'n' Roll Mentorship, baby! It is about rallying a legion of like-minded warriors who can jam together, challenge one another, and create history.

Think of the Industry Icon Program as your personal roadie to success.

Imagine a world where you are not just managing, but you are leading with flair, influencing with grace, and innovating like a boss. Sounds amazing, right? I designed the Industry Icon Program to do that just for you—a platform where the chords of ideas strike so harmoniously, they create a tune that is irresistibly captivating. It is where you enhance your influence, polish your personal brand, and add that special 'X' factor that makes you, well, iconic!

Similarly, let us look at my other community - The Game Changers. Picture a global stage lit up with the most incredible talents from across industries. My vision is to build more than just a network; it is a brotherhood and sisterhood of mavens, all riffing off each other's genius. Here, you are not just another cog in the wheel; you are part of an orchestra of excellence that celebrates collective crescendos and turns failures into stepping stones for jaw-dropping comebacks.

But why do you need this tribe, you might ask? Well, because even rock stars need a band and an audience. Having a community around you acts as your safety net and your cheer squad. They share your vision and speak your language, and when the chips are down, they are your backstage heroes, lifting you up, and pushing you to deliver that encore the world's been waiting for.

So, your opus work, your special symphony, may just be crafting your own concert by building and aligning supportive communities.

So, how does your organization join this global gig of greatness? Start by identifying the changemakers within your team. Unearth the hidden gems that resonate with your vision and are eager to make a big bang. From there, build a space—a jamming room, if you will—where these talents can collide, collaborate, and create the next big hit. Recognize and celebrate those little wins because they are the opening acts for the headlining success your community is bound to achieve.

So, there you have it! Ready to trade in that solo act for a chart-topping band? I designed The Industry Icon program and The Game Changers to be your VIP tickets to this epic concert of collaboration and success.

It was not merely about mentorship; it was about building a community of peers who understand, support, and challenge each other.

The Industry Icon program is designed to guide leaders in defining their personal brand, enhancing their influence, and fostering innovation. It is a platform where ideas are exchanged, strategies are developed, and success is celebrated.

The Game Changers, on the other hand, represents a global network of mavens striving to make a difference in their respective fields. It is a space for collaboration, inspiration, and collective growth.

What does your organization need to create similar like-minded supporting communities?

The New Headliners: Why Today's Business Leaders Are the Rock Stars of the Modern World

You see, there is a seismic shift happening right now—the people we look up to have changed. We have moved from stadium concerts to boardroom presentations. Yes, today's business leaders are the Mick Jaggers and David Bowies of our time. They are captivating, revolutionary, and man, do they know how to put on a show!

Consider Jeff Bezos—this guy did not just set up a shop; he orchestrated a retail revolution with Amazon. Angela Merkel? She is the Joan Jett of politics, wielding her influence to guide Germany through life's many mosh pits. Let us not forget Sundar Pichai. He is the rock god of technology, steering Google through the labyrinth of global complexities with the grace of a guitar solo that brings down the house.

But here is the kicker. When they strike the right chords, these are not just your run-of-the-mill celebrities. These new-age rock stars come equipped with a blueprint for success, a treasure chest of innovations, and a compass pointing the way for not just one industry but all of them. They are the genre-defying artists of the business world, breaking down barriers and setting trends faster than you can say "Encore!"

What sets these titans apart? They do not just read the room; they read the world. These leaders understand the pulse of the market, the rhythm of innovation, and the melody of consumer needs. They know when to smash that guitar and challenge the status quo and when to soothe the audience with a soul-stirring ballad of empathy and vision. They do not just adapt to change; they are the change. Let me tell you, that is the secret ingredient to their brand of stardom.

So, how do you join this hall of fame? Where is the roadmap to becoming the next visionary? This is precisely why programs like Industry Icon exist. They offer the stage, the setlist, and the crowd, helping you evolve from an opening act to the star of the show. It is about mastering the fine art of resonating with people—your staff, your clients, your industry—and inspiring a whole new wave of innovation.

It is your time to shine.

Remember, you have got all it takes to be the next big thing, the trailblazer everyone has got their eyes on. Do not settle for mediocrity when you can headline your own life and become a beacon for the world to follow.

The Global Jam Session: How Leadership Transcends Industry Boundaries

Whether you are a tech geek, a healthcare hero, or a Wall Street whiz, this tune is for you. Because the great thing about leadership—it is like music, universally awesome and does not care what label you slap on it!

First, let us give a shout-out to some of these universal superstars! Mary Barra, GM's rockstar CEO, did not just climb the corporate ladder; she electrified it! She is steering the behemoth of General Motors like a maestro conducting a symphony of electric vehicles. Then you have got Indra Nooyi. She turned PepsiCo into an eco-conscious, socially responsible powerhouse. It is like watching a lead guitarist transition from hard rock to acoustic flawlessly, right?

Kudos where it is due.

Now, here is where it gets mind-blowing. These incredible leaders are proving that you do not need to be confined to one industry to make waves. You could be a techno DJ in Silicon Valley or a soulful crooner in healthcare, and you would still rock just as hard. Why? Because leadership is the universal language of impact. It speaks to people, not just balance sheets or market segments.

So, what is the playlist for world-changing leadership? Well, it is composed of innovation, resilience, and the audacity to dream big. It is about identifying those raw, emotional chords that resonate with your audience—be it staff, clients, or the global community—and strumming them in a way that spurs action. The best part? When you hit the right notes, your influence reverberates far beyond your immediate sphere, contributing to a universal symphony of progress.

It is about creating your jamming studio, alongside your mentors, who also become your biggest fans. They help you find your unique rhythm, craft your lyrics of influence, and then belt them out in a way that makes the world sit up and listen.

The stage is set. The crowd is roaring, the spotlight is on, and the mic is all yours. Do not be confined by industry stereotypes. Let your leadership style be your signature tune that others want to cover. Whether you are in tech, healthcare, finance, or any other field, remember: You are not just here to play the game; you are here to change it.

The Art of Amplification through Building Influence: Writing, Speaking and Podcasting.

The great captains of industry also have an amazing playbook, and I do not mean just how they run companies. Nope, I am talking about how they run their influence game as if they are starring in their own rock opera!

Let us kick off with a toast to Sheryl Sandberg. She did not just climb to the top of the tech world; she authored her own soundtrack with "Lean In." And what a tune it has become—a rallying cry for women, a conversation starter, and yes, a movement. She is not alone. Today's CEOs are adding an author, podcaster, and motivational speaker to their ever-growing résumé of skills.

You can define your choice of instrument.

We are talking podcasts, keynote speeches, books, you name it! Leaders are realizing they've got an entire world stage to perform on. It is like when the lead guitarist of a legendary band decides to go solo and ends up chart-topping. You get to amplify your influence while rocking your company's goals. And the best part? You are not just talking to the C-suite or your staff; you are chatting with the entire world!

Let us rename the phrase Thought Leader and let us talk about the Thought Rockstar.

How do you make sure your voice is not just another blip on the radar? You build a brand around it! Much like iconic rock stars, your voice, your words, and your ideas should be as distinctive as your own autograph. That is what it means to be an Industry Icon. You are not just pushing a corporate agenda; you are penning the lyrics to the next generation's anthem of success!

But hey, even rock stars need their bands, right? That is where The Game Changers community comes in. Think of it as your jamming circle. It is a place where you can riff off each other's ideas, perfect your chords of influence, and even collaborate on world-changing hits. It is not a one-man show; it is a collective chorus of industry-defining brilliance.

Your influence should not just be a one-hit-wonder; it should be a legacy---a full album of hits that inspire innovation, shape the market, and create a mentorship chain that keeps on rocking! Your podcast can ignite a startup founder's light bulb moment. Your book might be the manual that fuels a social change movement. Your speech could be the motivational kick someone needs to skyrocket their career.

Sounds daunting? It is not really.

Just pick up that pen, hit that record button, and step onto that stage. Share your wisdom, fuel your industry's future, and let your voice reverberate across the globe.

Ready? Set. Go amplify!

In Conclusion: Your Legacy Awaits – Believe and Take Action

You, as a leader, as a visionary, already possess everything you need to make an indelible mark on the world. Your knowledge, your expertise, your passion – it is all there, waiting to be harnessed and shared.

But let us take a moment to ponder an essential truth: Growth happens through connection, through collaboration, through sharing our wisdom with others, and through the legacy you are destined to create? It is not a solitary endeavor. It is a journey enriched by those who benefit from your insights, your guidance, your innovation.

Imagine penning that book that will inspire generations. Think of launching a podcast that resonates with thousands, a platform where your voice is heard, your ideas are shared, and your strategies become the blueprint for success.

Now is the time to take that leap, to believe in yourself, and to recognize that your potential is boundless, and your influence is exponential. Your legacy is not merely a future promise; it is a living, breathing entity that begins with your action today.

Embrace the journey. Share your wisdom. Build connections. Let your legacy flourish and inspire others for many years to come.

The world is waiting for your brilliance, and let us be honest, so are you.

It is your time to discover how awesome you can truly be.

Time to jump and grow wings on the way down…

Coach MJ's Firepower Takeaways

- Rockin' the Boardroom: CEOs are the new rockstars, trading in guitars for spreadsheets, but still dropping legendary hits in the business world.

- Mic Drop Moments: Personal branding? It's your encore song! Branson, Winfrey – not just brands, but headlining icons. Your brand? Your leadership's greatest hit.

- The Universal Setlist: Leadership is the world's favorite tune, crossing genres from tech to healthcare, turning solo acts into global bands of changemakers.

- Crank Up the Volume: Today's top execs aren't just about memos. They're authoring, podcasting, speaking – amplifying influence to stadium-level crowds!

- Encore Awaits: Your legacy isn't just in the boardroom. It's in every word you share, every connection you make, and every leap you dare. The spotlight's on, and it's showtime!

Thank you, Dave!

“Attracting the Right Talent Wins Championships”

Coach M J Tolan

Coach M J Tolan is an Entrepreneur, TEDx Speaker, Award-winning author of “Executive Powers, Cracking the Code to Magnetic Leadership,” two-time Cancer Warrior/Survivor Advocate, and International Keynote Inspirational Speaker.

He is the Founder of the World Class Institute of Leadership and Innovation, Firepower Partners, Co-Founder of Time 4 Sharing Children’s Charity, host of ‘The Real Mission: I’M Possible Show’ Podcast and The Firepower C-Suite.

"It always seems impossible until it's done."

NELSON MANDELLA

Throughout my entrepreneurial journey, I have been fortunate enough to experience being involved in several 'Start-Ups.'

All of these required someone to sell something to someone.
Sales create revenue, the oxygen that keeps the companies alive and breathing.

One of my businesses started on a shoestring; it was a small sales and marketing team for direct sales. This team consisted of me and two others at the time, but we were armed with a vision. I had seen the fall of communism in countries like Hungary and Poland, which presented a timely opportunity.

I rushed into Poland without knowing a single person, or a word of Polish and set up shop on the biggest hunch of my entire life.

This was an all-in play, a classic 'burn your boats' move so winning and succeeding was my only option. Why? I had bet the farm, given up any chance of an income where I was in order to take that giant leap of faith… move to Poland in the middle of winter.

I rented a house for my little team and I with an 'outhouse', meaning it was a really cold shuffle every morning. Not many people spoke English so translators were essential.

We hired new salespeople every month who effectively could increase revenue for the business.

The mathematical equation for this business model was:

No Sales = No Cash = No Dinner.

Back then, if someone were to do anything other than sales or marketing in which their contribution could not be calculated and measured as increased revenue daily, we did not hire them.

Of course, we eventually had to add on administrative staff, what we considered staff overhead, but remained with a 'Hungry Lion' attitude that new fresh saline the business world, anything of value rarely occurs until someone buys a product or service that someone else is selling. The other side is if no one is buying what you are selling, then 'Houston, we have a problem.'

What we could predict from our process-driven business was that if we could provide the correct number of leads to our sales team, which was another magic trick in itself, we would have the result we expected. It was a percentage game if you will.

In the direct sales business, cold leads are sometimes frosty ice cold, so no one ever came to us to buy anything.

Our products and services were presented through public presentations and always with translators as we operated in foreign markets such as Poland, Russia, Lithuania Bahrain, Bulgaria, Lebanon to name just a few.

So, no, yours truly did not speak a word of any foreign language. Our team needed translators to partner with to let us speak with every potential customer. We were so helpless to navigate the local language that after work, we asked our translation team to help us do our grocery shopping or food hunting as it was actually in some countries.

As the founder and operator, soon after we got sales and marketing up and running, it was my job to be the entrepreneur and rise above the day-to-day operations of sales, translations, and currency exchange operations. I had to constantly ask myself how I could improve the business that I had created.

This was quintessentially Blue Ocean marketing. The fall of the Berlin Wall created an opportunity to move into the Commonwealth Independent States, also known as CIS countries or former Soviet Bloc, and set up operations before every competitor under the sun showed up.

There were, after all, millions of new customers, and an excellent opportunity to be the first in the market meant lower lead costs and higher margins. Market research was driving through a city and looking for satellite dishes and new cars, telling symbols of prosperity. Emerging Markets.

In the first 18 months, we assembled a team of over 150 people.

I wanted to open offices in new territories, but I quickly realized my most significant limitations were based on a need for more qualified talent. This hindered my capability of opening more offices in a new country, market, and city.

Who could lead my company's new office or country market if I could not trust anyone? It was complicated. I had family members embedded in the operation.

It was a matter of Trust.

My stubbornness/fear not to trust anyone else cost me millions eventually as it ultimately meant that I was a late-entry player into some emerging lucrative markets because I had refused to bring in any new talent that I had not trained or worked with.

I later discovered this is a prevalent phobia many businesses founders face. I had all offices run by family members.

Still, I had a vision that I could scale the business and expand exponentially.

If only.

So, my stellar growth had abruptly stopped because of my 'lack of trust' in other people who were not connected to me or my family. It takes courage to look at things from a different perspective. Had I not eventually done that, we would have remained a three-office wonder in a shrinking market. Getting the right talent to match our values, ethics, and vision was critical and now a mission priority.

The quantum shift I was forced to make in my limited thinking allowed me to recruit outside leaders who would allow me to grow and expand. Like so many others, I was influenced by the dynamics of professional sports teams and by how actively recruiting one key player could be a game-changer for an entire team.

To remind myself and anyone reading this chapter, I have added three short examples of how importing talent to a sports team changes the game.

In Soccer - Football - Messi the Miracle

Before the dawn of the Lionel Messi era, FC Barcelona was a well-regarded club but not quite the European powerhouse they would become. In the 2003-2004 season, the club finished a lackluster second in La Liga. It had been knocked out of the UEFA Champions League at the quarter-final stage. Fans were growing restless.

Enter Lionel Messi—a shy, diminutive teenager from Argentina with an otherworldly talent for dribbling past defenders as if they were traffic cones. Though he debuted in 2004, it was from the 2005-2006 season that Messi began to shine. His dazzling dribbles, miraculous goals, and the sheer vision he displayed on the field were nothing short of awe-inspiring.

The rest is history. With Messi as their backbone, Barcelona won numerous La Liga titles, Champions League trophies, and even won six awards and trophies in one season, becoming one of the most successful clubs in modern history. His influence was not just confined to the scoreline; he elevated the level of play of his teammates, making them look good and the team unstoppable. More recently, this same player was transferred to the Miami club in the US, and the impact was nothing short of explosive.

The Reign of King James: Cleveland Cavaliers' Story of Redemption in the NBA

The city of Cleveland had long been a laughing stock when it came to sports. Despite a passionate fan base, the Cavaliers hadn't won an NBA championship in their history. LeBron James, a native of Akron, Ohio, was drafted by the Cleveland Cavaliers in 2003. His presence immediately uplifted the team's performance, but despite his prodigious talent, the team couldn't win the championship.

LeBron left for Miami in 2010, and the Cavaliers slumped. However, when he returned in 2014, everything changed. With a renewed sense of purpose and an incredible skill set, he single-handedly turned the Cavs into a powerhouse. In the 2015-2016 NBA season, against all odds and facing the historically great Golden State Warriors, LeBron led the Cavaliers to their first NBA Championship, ending a 52-year championship drought for the city of Cleveland. In this case, the right talent didn't just win championships; it healed a city.

Sakic's Saga: The Colorado Avalanche's Uprising

In 1995, the Quebec Nordiques moved to Colorado and became the Avalanche. They were a decent team but hadn't made a significant mark in the National Hockey League (NHL). Recognizing the need for transformational talent, they acquired Joe Sakic. With a keen eye for the game and leadership qualities to boot, Sakic was exactly what the Avalanche needed.

In his first season with the team, Sakic led them to their first Stanley Cup, defeating the Florida Panthers in an epic showdown. His contribution wasn't just in goals and assists; Sakic was a leader in the locker room, and his passion for the game was infectious. He elevated everyone around him, turning a decent team into champions. Sakic later became one of the greatest players in NHL history and was inducted into the Hall of Fame.

There are many more examples of how importing the right talent changed the fortune of teams.

Having this Eureka light go off in my head was a massive game-changer for my own business. Once I cracked the code, I was off to the races and scaled the company accordingly.

So, yes, I am glad I shifted my thinking. I am glad I opened my mind to importing sales leaders to new offices who were not related to the family.

Why?

Within 12 years, that little business I had started had chalked up sales of over 100,000,000 dollars.

This only happened by adding the right talent, the right faces in the right places.

Thankfully, my limited thinking changed enough for me to devote myself to finding a process to effectively recruit, onboard, and monitor new leaders who could take the baton and grow a new business territory.

Remember that not every candidate we sought to become our next 'Sales Director' had a burning desire to work in Beirut, Lebanon.

This was another hurdle.

Logic would say, why not hire someone within that country's market?

However, the extremely specific skill sets required only existed in the US.

Recruiting someone to leave their cozy life in Miami to take a chance on a new job in Kaliningrad, Russia, was a hard sell. The lifestyle offering was a negative 500%.

In each country, there were new languages, laws, currency restrictions, new housing issues, office practices, cultural observations, as well as customer service requirements and limitations.

Finding the right talent was not a cookie-cutter formula. It took a great deal of effort, and eventually, I took it upon myself to be the chief recruiter and trainer for my own business.

Recruiting salespeople from other countries requires high energy and a constant rinse and repeat. I interviewed thousands of candidates through seminars and one-on-one interviews until I finally divested, whereby the head count for sales and marketing was just north of 690 people wearing our logo.

I discovered that attracting, engaging, and training my teams brought me more personal satisfaction than any other job I had ever done.

For me, it was that 'Eureka' moment when recruits simultaneously got the message and the mission. After this, provide supportive encouragement and coaching to guide them through their personal empowerment highway and watch them get off to the races.

After divesting my interest in the business, I went on to establish the World Class Institute of Leadership and Innovation, which has been a Learning and Development (L&D) business unit since 2012.

It was here that I developed the expanded version of my 'Mission: I'M Possible' series of keynotes and workshops.

Igniting team performance requires an orchestrated partnership between the company client, their leadership, our state-of-the-art development programs, and execution management.

Our wheelhouse has been leadership and sales development training programs internationally.

Why?

The number of companies who focus on replacing staff who are leaving often fail to check if they have a cultural hole in the boat.

How to seal the leak?

This comes down to leadership accountability, awareness, the ability to engage teams, providing a culture where team members are encouraged to prosper and grow.

This phenomenon of companies 'ignoring the hole in the boat' provoked me to write 'Executive Powers, Cracking the Code to Magnetic Leadership'.

As an entrepreneur I felt a more respectful leadership model which incorporated empathy and self-awareness was now needed more than ever.

It still is.

As seasoned recruiters of sales talent in multiple industries for decades, we strategically leveraged our executive search experience to complement our learning and development activities.

The evolution of attracting talent to companies has made a quantum leap with modern technology tools available today.

The advent of new technologies has dramatically transformed the talent acquisition landscape, enabling companies to make quantum leaps in how they attract, assess, and retain top-notch personnel.

One of the most powerful "secret weapons" in this high-stakes competitive arena is the use of specialized executive search firms.

Coupled with their industry reputation and cutting-edge tech tools, these firms offer a way for companies not just to keep pace with the competition but transcend ahead.

Supercharged Speed and Scalability

Automated screening tools, AI algorithms, and chatbots have exponentially increased the speed and efficiency of the initial stages of the recruitment process. By taking on the heavy lifting of screening and initial assessments, companies are free to focus on a shortlist of highly qualified candidates, usually curated by their executive search partners.

Precision Targeting for Elite Roles

Executive search firms deploy multinational research teams and utilize machine learning and predictive algorithms to find candidates who not only have the requisite skills but also align with a company's strategic vision and culture.

By accurately targeting candidates for C-level and other senior roles, these firms give companies a leg up in acquiring the industry's best talent instantly ready to face the market, thus potentially leapfrogging competitors in terms of leadership quality and growth.

Expansive Outreach and Deep Engagement

While AI and social media have broadened the outreach of talent acquisition strategies, executive search firms offer the specificity and nuance that technology alone can't provide. They tap into exclusive networks and utilize insider knowledge to present opportunities that candidates might not find through traditional channels.

Virtual Assessment, Real Results

Tools for video interviewing and virtual onboarding expand the pool of accessible talent to global dimensions. Executive search firms often facilitate these virtual interfaces, ensuring that both parties can effectively assess each other, even from thousands of miles apart.

The Data-Driven Advantage

Real-time and predictive analytics provide invaluable insights into recruitment effectiveness, time-to-hire, and other crucial metrics. Executive search firms can help interpret this data and realign strategies to capture the best talent before the competition even identifies them as prospects.

Building a Diverse and Inclusive Future

The importance of diversity and inclusion can't be overstated. Blind recruitment tools and algorithms can present a more diverse pool of candidates. Nonetheless, it is the executive search firms, with their industry relationships and extensive databases, that can convert this into actionable hires at the senior levels.

Enhancing Candidate Experience & Retention

The candidate's experience from initial contact through onboarding sets the stage for long-term retention. Executive search firms often manage this intricate process, ensuring that candidates are not only well-suited for the role but are also committed for the long haul.

Long-Term Strategic Partnership

Executive search firms are shifting from transactional to more retainer-based models, fostering long-term relationships. This aligns their success with the company's, forming a strategic partnership not just to fill roles but also to contribute to long-term growth and competitive advantage.

By integrating cutting-edge technology tools with the specialized services of executive search firms, companies can create a potent combination to identify, woo, and retain top-tier talent. This blend of tech and specialized expertise forms a secret weapon, enabling companies to leapfrog their competition and position themselves as leaders in their respective industries.

"Great entrepreneurs know a secret to growing a successful business is much like being a top movie director or successful sports team owner...

...always attract the best talent you can find for the win!"

Having the right talent on your leadership team can be an absolute game-changer.

The company that secures the best talent first is King.

It's your move.

Coach MJ's Firepower Takeaways

Leap into the Unknown: Who would've thought that venturing into a chilly Polish winter without knowing a single word would lead to a business empire? It's a vivid testament: sometimes, the path less traveled, however frosty, is paved with gold!

The Trust Equation: Ever thought your inability to trust could cost you millions? As the narrative unfolds, we learn the weighty price of playing it too safe. Broadening your inner circle can mean broadening your horizons.

Scouting for Business 'Messi's': From the soccer fields of Barcelona to the boardrooms of multinational firms, the magic ingredient remains consistent: unparalleled talent. One game-changing recruit can redefine the destiny of an entire organization.

The Perfect Blend: In our tech-savvy age, weaving together the precision of AI with the human expertise of executive search firms emerges as the secret recipe for success. It's a beautiful dance of numbers and intuition.

Beyond the Horizon: When there's a gap, bridge it. From cultural nuances to language barriers, the story reaffirms that with the right mindset and talent, obstacles turn into stepping stones. And as you turn the last page, remember: every challenge is but an invitation to create a riveting success story!

Thank you from our Sponsors

Firepower Talent Partners serves business clients through its Four Pillars of excellence: Learning and Development, Talent Search, International Consulting, and C-level Executive Coaching.

If you would like to explore how your organization could get to the next level and get in touch with any of our co-authors/board advisors:

Visit: http://www.Unleashingfirepower.com

Firepower Talent Partners and Coach MJ Tolan will devote a portion of all profits to Children with Cancer in the Philippines.

Made in the USA
Columbia, SC
07 July 2025